THE LAYMAN'S BIBLE COMMENTARY

THE LAYMAN'S BIBLE COMMENTARY
IN TWENTY-FIVE VOLUMES

THE LAYMAN'S
BIBLE COMMENTARY

Balmer H. Kelly, *Editor*

Donald G. Miller *Associate Editors* **Arnold B. Rhodes**

Dwight M. Chalmers, *Editor, John Knox Press*

VOLUME 13

THE BOOK OF
EZEKIEL

THE BOOK OF
DANIEL

Carl G. Howie

JOHN KNOX PRESS
ATLANTA, GEORGIA

Published in Great Britain by SCM Press Ltd., London.

Fifth printing 1975

Complete set: ISBN: 0-8042-3026-9
This volume: 0-8042-3013-7
Library of Congress Card Number: 59-10454
Printed in the United States of America

PREFACE

The LAYMAN'S BIBLE COMMENTARY is based on the conviction that the Bible has the Word of good news for the whole world. The Bible is not the property of a special group. It is not even the property and concern of the Church alone. It is given to the Church for its own life but also to bring God's offer of life to all mankind —wherever there are ears to hear and hearts to respond.

It is this point of view which binds the separate parts of the LAYMAN'S BIBLE COMMENTARY into a unity. There are many volumes and many writers, coming from varied backgrounds, as is the case with the Bible itself. But also as with the Bible there is a unity of purpose and of faith. The purpose is to clarify the situations and language of the Bible that it may be more and more fully understood. The faith is that in the Bible there is essentially one Word, one message of salvation, one gospel.

The LAYMAN'S BIBLE COMMENTARY is designed to be a concise non-technical guide for the layman in personal study of his own Bible. Therefore, no biblical text is printed along with the comment upon it. This commentary will have done its work precisely to the degree in which it moves its readers to take up the Bible for themselves.

The writers have used the Revised Standard Version of the Bible as their basic text. Occasionally they have differed from this translation. Where this is the case they have given their reasons. In the main, no attempt has been made either to justify the wording of the Revised Standard Version or to compare it with other translations.

The objective in this commentary is to provide the most helpful explanation of fundamental matters in simple, up-to-date terms. Exhaustive treatment of subjects has not been undertaken.

In our age knowledge of the Bible is perilously low. At the same time there are signs that many people are longing for help in getting such knowledge. Knowledge of and about the Bible is, of course, not enough. The grace of God and the work of the Holy Spirit are essential to the renewal of life through the Scriptures. It is in the happy confidence that the great hunger for the Word is a sign of God's grace already operating within men, and that the Spirit works most wonderfully where the Word is familiarly known, that this commentary has been written and published.

THE EDITORS AND
THE PUBLISHERS

THE BOOK OF

EZEKIEL

INTRODUCTION

The Book Itself

The Book of Ezekiel, emerging out of one of the most creative
eras of human history—the great divide of pre-exilic and post-
exilic faith—is basic to the understanding of God's movements
and meaning in history. At the same time it is one of the longest
and most bewildering parts of the Old Testament. A major
prophet, in length and in importance for our understanding of the
revelation of God, Ezekiel combines the bizarre with the enigmatic, making interpretation very difficult. This prophet is, himself, no easy personality to fathom, being given to the most aston-
ishingly eccentric activity.

The book as we have it has usually been equally divided into
(1) prophecies of doom, before the fall of Jerusalem (chs. 1-24)
and (2) prophecies of hope, after the fall of Jerusalem (chs. 25-
48). However, like most simplifications, this is an oversimplifica-
tion and, as such, is misleading. In general, the first half of the
book (chs. 1-24) should be set chronologically before the fall of
Jerusalem in 587 B.C., when the general theme is doom, although
a ray of hope occasionally breaks through. Chapters 25-32 are
concerned with prophecies against foreign nations, with but one
intrusion about Judah. Then there follows a conglomerate series
of visions and oracles of promise and hope in chapters 33-39. The
last grand piece consists of a vision of the Temple restored, portraying in extensive detail the structure of the Temple, rules for
its use, and a restored society.

Authorship and Date

The Book of Ezekiel, according to substantial and persistent
tradition, is the product of a prophet whose name is attached

to the book and who was carried captive when the Jews were exiled by Nebuchadnezzar in 598 B.C. This view is strongly held in the present because this strangely fascinating book seems to fit well into the era to which tradition has consistently assigned it. It was a time when individual security and corporate existence, both political and religious, were in jeopardy.

Suggestions that an unknown author composed the book as a piece of pure fiction during the waning years of Israel are not substantiated by the evidence. To question not only authorship by Ezekiel but his existence itself is to ignore his secure place in history. The matter of authorship must be discussed together with date, hence we turn to dating of the prophecy. At this juncture we shall not concern ourselves with late editorial additions, if there are such; rather, our first interest is in the main body of the book.

Ezekiel, the son of a priest and perhaps himself a priest, recalls in some detail the dimensions of the Solomonic Temple, which becomes the unconscious, visionary model for his Temple of the future (chs. 40-42). A creative mind, remembering the familiar structure in whose shadow he had grown up, fashioned the vision of a Temple restored on the basis of the Temple which had been destroyed. Such a person necessarily lived before the fall of the city in 587 B.C. when the Solomonic Temple was utterly ruined.

The prophet, who was meticulous about remembering when major events of vision or fact happened, gives thirteen definite dates in his book. In the first three verses, two dates have become mixed, probably as a result of later compilation of the entire book by Ezekiel himself. The whole scheme of dating must be understood as a single system, and the "thirtieth year" (1:1) should be interpreted in that light. Dates are fixed according to the reign of Jehoiachin, who, though taken captive in the third month of his reign, was in all probability still considered the legitimate ruler. Furthermore, the beginning of his rule coincided with the beginning of the Captivity, so the Jews were able to speak of the years of captivity but at the same time to have in mind the regnal years of their deposed, legitimate monarch. To acknowledge openly the continued valid rule of Jehoiachin would have been considered revolt, but by this ruse the same effect was accomplished.

The "thirtieth year" does not refer to the age of the prophet; it is rather the year in which Ezekiel and his disciples gathered together his oracles into a single scroll. In the light of this suggestion, the following arrangement of dates appears to be correct:

Reference	Day	Month	Year	Event
1:1	5	4	30	Compilation of prophecy
1:2	5	—	5	Inaugural vision
8:1	5	6	6	Visions of the Temple
20:1	10	5	7	Warnings of history
24:1	10	10	9	The siege begun
26:1	1	—	11	Oracle against Tyre
29:1	12	10	10	Oracle against Egypt
30:20	7	1	11	Oracle against Pharaoh
31:1	1	3	11	Oracle against Pharaoh
32:1	1	12	12	Dirge over Pharaoh
32:17	15	1	12	Egypt dead
33:21	5	10	12	Jerusalem fallen
40:1	10	—	25	Vision of the future

Except for the dates attached to the foreign nations section, chapters 25-32, we may confidently assume that the definite chronological order is a part of the original work, which will be discussed later. It is possible that the dates for the oracles against Tyre (26:1) and Egypt (29:1, 17; 30:20; 31:1; 32:17) were added at the time of the compilation of the book in order to fit the foreign nations material into the regular chronological scheme, but this is hypothetical. In any case, these dates are probably correct. There is a natural and logical progression of dates—with the possible exception of dates for the foreign nations passages—from the inaugural vision to the fall of the city to the vision of the Temple restored.

However, not all the material placed between any two dates mentioned in the book necessarily belongs there chronologically. This is especially true of the date in 8:1. Ezekiel remembered and dated his inaugural vision and call (1:2; 3:16); his vision of the degraded Temple practice was an unforgettable experience (8:1); his encounter with religious leaders was a memorable event (20:1); and the beginning of the siege was etched deep and dark in memory (24:1), connected as it was with the death of his wife. News of Jerusalem's fall (33:21), which should be placed in the eleventh year, not the twelfth, was a climactic and tragic occasion which led ultimately to the grand vision and promise of the land restored (40:1). Apparently the prophet, when he or his disciples compiled the book, used such a chronological framework, but in

the case of 8:1 a vision led to the collection of oracles of indictment against Jerusalem. Having remembered the vision, the
prophet collected those oracles which vindicated God's justice,
oracles related to one another in subject matter rather than in
time of delivery. In some such manner the work of a great prophet
who lived in the sixth century was brought near to completion.

Ezekiel was a man of his times who was careful to leave obvious dates for posterity, but who also indirectly manifested ideas,
knowledge, and attitudes which irrevocably place him in the sixth
century B.C. This was a time of great social, political, and spiritual
flux that could have become either the basis for new creative understanding of the place of God in the life of men or the dying
gasp of an inadequate faith. It was largely due to Ezekiel and Second Isaiah that out of the ashes of destruction came the resurrection of new faith and hope.

Historical Background and Locale for the Prophecy

The age in which Ezekiel prophesied saw the dissolution of
the Assyrian Empire with the capture of Asshur in 614 B.C. and
the fall of Nineveh in 612 B.C. The *coup de grâce* was admin-
istered at Carchemish when Nebuchadnezzar, the son of the Chaldean Nabopolassar, crushed the Assyrian forces and turned his
attention to Egypt. Rumblings of revolt and discontent reached a
climax long before these stirring events, with the rise to power of
Nabopolassar about 625 B.C., when the last great Assyrian monarch, Asshurbanipal, died. That year Nabopolassar declared himself king of Babylon, and the Assyrians were powerless to deny
his claim. Not even the ill-fated intervention of Pharaoh Neco
around 609 B.C. and later at Carchemish in 605 B.C. could stem
the Chaldean tide. Assyria, long a monolithic landmark in the
ancient world, was no more; in her place stood Nebuchadnezzar,
the Chaldean, who began to build the neo-Babylonian Empire
(625-539 B.C.).

Within Judah itself, the age of Manasseh (687-642 B.C.) had
seen religious syncretism reach a flood tide which was more or
less inevitable. In spite of the deliverance of Jerusalem from Sen-
nacherib in 701 B.C., when Isaiah was prophet, Judah remained
a vassal of the Assyrian Empire. It is probable that the Assyrian
legions returned a few years later and successfully subdued the
city. Be that as it may, political vassalage also meant religious

subservience. During this period of darkness, prophetic voices were silent and the record states, "Moreover Manasseh shed very much innocent blood, till he had filled Jerusalem from one end to another" (II Kings 21:16).

After Amon's brief reign, a boy king named Josiah, who apparently had been profoundly influenced by the prophetic party, took the throne (about 640-639 B.C.). In his eighteenth year (II Kings 22:3), while the Temple was being rehabilitated, a scroll of the Law was found which, in the name of God, commanded observance of long neglected and forgotten practices. It is probable that the scroll found in this manner consisted, in the main, of Deuteronomy 12-26, and that it is an interpretation of the Mosaic Law composed during an earlier reform under Hezekiah, less than a century before. The scroll, having been judged authentic by Huldah the prophetess, became the basis for a reform, instituted by Josiah, which attempted to accomplish two things: (1) to centralize worship in Jerusalem and (2) to rid the country of all syncretistic cults. Apparently this reform met with initial success, thanks to the royal will and power to purge dissident elements, and thanks also to the popular fear of foreign attack (see II Kings 22-23).

However, the reform was dealt a deathblow when Josiah attempted to intercept the forces of Pharaoh Neco at Megiddo in 609 B.C. Whether the king had a misguided sense of the inviolability of the Holy Land or whether his was a military miscalculation is not known to us. In fact, it is possible that Josiah never managed to fight a battle with Pharaoh Neco but was summarily executed when he appeared to negotiate with the Egyptian invader. Whatever the fact of this matter, the corpse of the king was the symbol and signal that his reform was at an end.

After Josiah the throne of Judah changed hands rapidly. Jehoahaz was chosen by the people as ruler, but this choice was vetoed three months later by the Egyptians, who elevated Jehoiakim to the throne (609-598 B.C.). When the battle of Carchemish was over and the Egyptians were beating a hasty retreat homeward, the king of Judah found little difficulty in switching his loyal vassalage to Nebuchadnezzar and the Chaldeans (605 B.C.). Rebellion against these same Chaldeans three years later finally brought the force of Chaldean arms against Jerusalem itself. Jehoiakim died during the siege. His ill-starred successor and son Jehoiachin, after a three months' reign, surrendered the city to the Chaldeans and went with the prominent people of the land into captivity. It was in this group that Ezekiel made the long eight-hundred-mile trek to the Mesopotamian valley where he lived in Tel-abib on the Chebar Canal.

Life continued in Jerusalem, even though the city was depopulated of its leaders. Mattaniah, who took the throne name Zedekiah, a brother of Jehoiakim, ascended the throne in 597 B.C. For about eight years his vassalage to Nebuchadnezzar was complete, so outward harmony continued. Yet in these years, as is plainly stated in Jeremiah and Ezekiel, there was a tug of war in Judah between parties favoring Egyptian domination in place of neo-Babylonian control. Revolt came in the year 590 B.C. and the city of Jerusalem was soon besieged. A brief foray by Pharaoh Hophra caused the siege to be lifted momentarily, giving rise to false hopes among the inhabitants of the land, but inevitably the end came in 587 B.C. when the city fell. Zedekiah's attempt at escape failed. After he had seen his two sons executed, his eyes were gouged out. What happened to the blinded king after this tragic incident is not known.

Gedaliah was quickly established as ruler of the ruined state, but he was treacherously murdered by Ishmael, a fellow countryman; and with that, all semblance of limited local autonomy ceased in Judah. Thus the real center of Jewish life and mission was shifted to the exiles in Tel-abib and possibly in other Mesopotamian areas as well.

Where does Ezekiel fit into the picture? He has already been identified, in accordance with well-established tradition, as a prophet among the exiles. Yet this conclusion is not without its problems. A prophet, overwhelmed by a vision in Mesopotamia, is called to speak God's word of judgment to a rebellious nation eight hundred miles distant. If Ezekiel remained in Mesopotamia for his entire ministry, he must have had a most unusual career, and apparently possessed extrasensory powers.

The prophet is commissioned to speak to "the house of Israel" (for example, 3:16-21; 18:1-32; 33:1-20) and is told on several occasions to address the people of Judah and the inhabitants of Jerusalem (12:10-11; 16:2). Prophecies to a rebellious house still in Judah would appear to be highly irrelevant to the exiles in Babylonia, and several references actually place Ezekiel in Jerusalem (21:1). For a man living in Mesopotamia he commands a remarkably intimate and detailed knowledge of events in Jerusalem as they happened, and he carries out prophetic acts which would have real significance only in Jerusalem (for example, in chs. 4 and 12). Finally, to place Ezekiel in Palestine, where he would seem to be, removes any necessity for ascribing extra-sensory powers to him. At first glance these considerations seem very formidable and have caused many to deny that Ezekiel's entire ministry was spent among the exiles at Tel-abib.

Four alternate possibilities have been put forward in place of the traditional view. (1) Ezekiel had a vision in Mesopotamia but received a call to return to Palestine, in 593 B.C. He obeyed the call, returned to Jerusalem and prophesied until 587 B.C. when the city fell, whereupon he returned to Tel-abib and completed his ministry. (2) Ezekiel's entire prophetic ministry was spent in Palestine; he never went to Babylonia; the Babylonian locale is to be accounted for as the result of editorial additions to the book. (3) Ezekiel received his call to prophesy in Jerusalem and pursued that calling until the siege of the city began. During the siege he moved to a nearby village where he received news of the city's fall, after which he went to Babylonia where he exercised the remainder of his ministry. (4) Ezekiel is a fictional person whose locale is not an important matter of historical fact.

As impressive as some of these alternatives may seem, they raise more problems than they settle. That Ezekiel was in Mesopotamia is demonstrated by numerous features of the book. Place names in Ezekiel have now been identified in inscriptions from the Mesopotamian valley. A canal, "Chebar," has been identified and "Tel-abib" is the Hebrew equivalent of the Assyrian name, "ruin of Abubu." Low conical hillocks were thought to be ruins from the Great Deluge sent by Abubu, the storm god. Ezekiel lived on such a ruined mound near the Chebar Canal. Neither of these places can any longer be passed over as the figment of some fertile imagination. In addition to these facts, there are numerous references to a Babylonian residence which can be removed only on the basis of a preconceived notion.

In 4:1 there is found a term which means "mud brick," on which a map of the city was scratched. In chapter 12 the prophet is told to "dig" through the wall. In addition to these items there is the wall described in chapter 13 which has been repaired with whitewash and which will fall when rain comes. Such usages point most definitely, not to the hill country of Judah, but to the adobe and mud-brick structures in Mesopotamia, where such structures were common and where the practice of drawing a city's map on a mud brick was widespread. Another topographical reference also points to a Mesopotamian locale, namely, the use of "plain" (3:22; literally, "wide valley"), the kind common to Mesopotamia (see Gen. 11:2).

In addition to these inadvertent Babylonian fingerprints, the explanation that the prophet was called not to "a people of foreign speech and a hard language" (3:5) would have little point outside a foreign land. If Ezekiel lived where the prevalent language was foreign to him this explanation makes sense. Such a call is more likely to have been heard by the River Chebar than in Jerusalem.

Ezekiel, being resident among the exiles, was in fact a prophet to one people, separated by space only. He kept in general touch with the situation in Jerusalem prior to 587 B.C. and most assuredly had knowledge of what was going on from memory of the city, its common life and institutions. In fact, when he went to the city in vision, he usually had the kind of experience which one might expect from visionary rather than actual contact. Even so, these visions of the Temple and Jerusalem (chs. 8 and 11) certainly reflect in some measure real conditions prevailing in the city.

Living among the exiles, who expected to return momentarily to Jerusalem, it was important that Ezekiel emphasize in word and act that there would be no immediate return from captivity. Thus, by his oracles against faraway Jerusalem, and by his dramatic acts, he sought to destroy any false optimism among the exiles and began to build a firm base for the harsh realities ahead. Once news of Jerusalem's fall reached him, he was no longer concerned primarily with vindicating God's honor. At that point in his ministry he turned his attention to the hope which God promised his people, and to the certainty of national revival.

Having said these things, let us be quite sure that the prophet was speaking to two audiences in the early years of his ministry, one in Palestine, the other in Babylonia. He spoke directly to the people at Tel-abib, but his words found their way back to Jerusalem, since movement between the two places was not impossible (see Jer. 29). Thus the prophetic word became a creative agent for despair or hope, whether spoken directly or indirectly.

Ezekiel the Man

A brief word about the prophet himself is necessary, because he has been the subject of much distortion. That Ezekiel was not what we should consider a "normal person" is admitted, but his abnormality is a key to his greatness, as has been the case with many of history's notable personalities.

In the first place, Ezekiel carried out a number of ecstatic and dramatic acts which conveyed to his audience his prophetic message (for example, 3:25-26; 4:1-15; 5:1-4; 12:3-7; 12:17; 24: 3-5; 24:15-18; 37:15-17). Symbolic acts, such as eating food in the manner of people under siege and rehearsing an escape from the city, reinforced the communication of words. Similar ecstatic and symbolic acts had long been a part of the regular prophetic experience.

A most persistent question has arisen because of Ezekiel's incredible capacity for spiritual movement from one place to another (Chaldea to Jerusalem), followed by a speedy return to normal life. His ability to identify himself with the other exiles at Tel-abib and then return to a normal role demonstrates that he was in no sense a schizoid personality. Instead he is best understood as a sensitive human soul caught in the crosscurrents of history, driven by a burning zeal for God, painfully aware of the tragedy in which his people were involved.

Ezekiel's seems at first to be a harsh ministry, but zeal to vindicate God and to preserve a remnant for mission proves him to have been guided by profound insight. Among the truly great men of God stands this strange, contradictory figure whose creative spirit, energized by God, helped return the main stream of religion to the proper channel of mission.

Literary Form of the Book

This prophetic work contains some of the finest poetry in all the Old Testament, but alongside the poetry stands cumbersome and colorless prose. Few passages in the Old Testament reach such heights of poetic beauty as passages in the oracles against Tyre and Egypt (chs. 26-32); there is sheer ecstatic beauty in the song of the sword (21:8-17) and in the dramatic exultation over the vindication of the Lord (6:11b-12).

The book bristles with problems and is possibly honeycombed with short editorial additions, but, over all, there is a unity of vocabulary and point of view. Apocalyptic passages such as chapters 9, 37, and 38-39 have become models for later literature. The features of the vision in chapter 1 have reappeared many times in the later symbolism of both Judaism and Christianity.

Parables, many of them possibly drawn from the folklore of the people, are tellingly used by the prophet. The parable of the vine (ch. 15) is followed by the magnificent parable of the deserted child beloved of a stranger (ch. 16). Parables of two eagles (ch. 17), of a lioness and her young lions (ch. 19), of two scarlet sisters (ch. 23), and of a caldron (ch. 24) add richness to this great work.

Most of chapter 10, which is largely a repetition of chapter 1, was probably added by later editors as was chapter 33, but both chapters are in keeping with Ezekiel's own work. It is also quite probable that parts of chapters 43-46 are a later expansion of the grand vision of the future (chs. 40-48), since they reflect the priestly attitude of a later day. Other shorter sections will be discussed as they arise, but suffice it to say here that even the elements not directly from the prophet came for the most part from his close followers. Except for brief editorial accretions, the book is from the prophet Ezekiel's hand or arises out of the implications of his teachings.

The Message of the Book

No new major theological themes are created by the prophet, but the profound doctrines of the Old Testament are reinforced and clarified by him. God is shown to be the key to life; the arena for revelation is history; the Lord is a God of nations and yet is above nations. These great themes are presented and specific problems are broached—for example, the relationship of individual responsibility to corporate guilt and the shape of a reconstituted society. Most important of all, amid the harshness of judgment the gracious love of God is manifest.

God Is the Key to Life

In the Covenant, God had agreed to be a God to Israel and the Israelites had promised to be his people. By means of law and prophetic teaching, what it meant to be the People of God had been clearly detailed. Reference to the sojourn in Egypt and to the wandering in the wilderness proved that their forefathers had become a people only because God was the creative force and the unifying presence in their midst. Symbolically he was at the center of the nation. Life depended on his presence. His glory remained only so long as the atmosphere of life provided a setting befitting it. In Jerusalem and Judah his continued presence was out of the question on account of the sorry record of Covenant-breaking. God was forced to withdraw, and the city was doomed.

But even as doom and death were signaled by the divine withdrawal, so resurrection and hope were based on the return of God's Spirit. Four passages underscore the fact that God is the key to life: the allegory of the Shepherd (34:11-31), the vision of dry bones (37:1-14), the figure of the river proceeding from the Temple (47:1-12), and the name of the restored city ("The LORD is there," 48:35). The secret of renewal, the only ground of hope, is the presence of God in the life of man (48:35b).

The Arena of Revelation Is History

Once more the theme is not new, but it receives added emphasis through the tragic events of history. Again and again the actions of the Almighty are explained as basically revelatory in nature; that is to say, their chief purpose is to reveal to mankind through illustrative events what kind of God the Lord is. His fury against the city of Jerusalem is explained with the phrase, "they shall know that I, the LORD, have spoken in my jealousy" (5:13b). He is one who will brook no rival. Furthermore, the Exile itself is given a similar purpose: "But I will let a few of them escape from the sword, from famine and pestilence, that they may confess all their abominations among the nations where they go, and may know that I am the LORD" (12:16).

However, God is not only known in judgment; he is also encountered in gracious renewal, as is evidenced in 16:62 and 20:44 where divine grace renews the Covenant and does not visit Judah's evil ways upon her. When the earth is made new and a blissful age has been initiated in Palestine, it is said, "They shall know that I am the LORD, when I break the bars of their yoke, and deliver them from the hand of those who enslaved them" (34:27b). Most amazing among the demonstrations of God is the resuscitation in the valley of dry bones. There the word is definite, "And you shall know that I am the LORD, when I open your graves, and raise you from your graves, O my people" (37:13).

God Is the God of All Nations

Like all aspects of Hebrew faith, this insight was not reached by logical deduction, and in no sense is it to be considered a theological dogma. In experience the prophet not only beheld the mobile throne of the Almighty in Mesopotamia; he also watched great nations such as Tyre and Egypt under the judgment of God. Not even the pride of Tyre would be countenanced, nor would the power of Egypt deliver her from divine judgment. God is the God of all nations. Political states like Ammon, Moab, Edom, and Philistia, which had been the instruments of God's judgment, were now themselves to be destroyed for their sins. God is the Judge of all men and nations; his realm reaches far beyond the bounds of Palestine, and his power is effectual everywhere.

Individual Responsibility and Corporate Guilt

Chapter 18 and a shorter section in 33:10-20 have long been identified as the area of Ezekiel's most profound contribution to Hebrew thought. Actually, Ezekiel was dealing with an immediate problem of fact which had arisen among his fellow exiles, namely, the problem of inherited and corporate guilt. The prophet's answer to the theological riddle was simple: "The soul that sins shall die" (18:20). He maintained that the sins of the fathers are not visited on the sons and that the sins of the sons are not visited on the fathers. Every man is on his own. The prophet does not settle the problem of corporate guilt, but he does set in clear terms the fact that man is always responsible. Corporate guilt or inherited sin can never be used as excuse for blaming our predicament on God. Ezekiel did provide the way for a man to live in communion with God even though the Temple was wrecked and the nation destroyed. The individual was responsible but God did not desire that one person should die.

The Shape of the Reconstituted State

Ezekiel's vision of a New Israel was unique. Up to his time the old society had been very real and very visible—in a land, with a government and a Temple. Now those historic realities were swept away. What the prophet saw was a land physically revived, made fertile, and renewed in every sense. Furthermore, it was not enough for Judah to be brought back to life; the whole of Israel was to be reconstituted in Palestine, with the twelve tribes being given their rightful portions of land. In the midst of the land the Temple would be built within the domain of the true prince and the inheritance of priests and Levites. Here sacrifices would be made by the sons of Zadok only, and the Levites would be Temple servants. Ritual purity would be maintained, and contamination would be impossible since Gentiles were forbidden entrance.

The Gracious Goodness of God

Some have denied to Ezekiel any passage which carries a breath of hope. Yet to excise all the passages wherein God in his grace forgives and restores, would destroy the book. God promises to redeem human nature itself by giving to man a new heart and a new spirit to replace the old heart of stone and the spirit of rebellion (18:31; 36:26). Moreover, one seems to hear an echo of Hosea in the agonized word of God, "For I have no pleasure in the death of anyone, says the Lord GOD; so turn, and live" (18:32).

All the way through the prophecy, God's gracious purpose to preserve a remnant for himself through his love is never forgotten. In 6:8-10; 14:21-23; and other more indirect references the promise appears. Restoration is a constant assumption, for by this time one could not really conceive of God as completely giving over his people to final destruction (see 16:50-63; 20:40-44; 36:22-38). But most important, the Covenant of God is an everlasting Covenant which is not to be easily cast aside. In this light the Exile must be interpreted as a purging process, that the purpose of the Covenant may be fulfilled.

OUTLINE

Prophecies of Doom Before the Fall of Jerusalem. Ezekiel 1:1—24:27

Vision and Call (1:1—3:27)
Visions and Oracles of Judgment (4:1—7:27)
Visions of the Prophet (8:1—11:25)
Prophecies Against Jerusalem (12:1—19:14)
Prophecies Against the Land (20:1—24:27)

Prophecies Against Foreign Nations. Ezekiel 25:1—32:32

Immediate Neighbors of Judah (25:1-17)
Tyre (26:1—28:23)
Editorial Interlude: Restoration of Israel (28:24-26)
Egypt (29:1—32:32)

Prophecies of Hope. Ezekiel 33:1—39:29

Editorial Review of Former Oracles (33:1-33)
Future Promise (34:1—37:28)
Gog and Magog (38:1—39:29)

The Temple and the City of God. Ezekiel 40:1—48:35

Measurement of the Temple (40:1—42:20)
Appearance of the Glory of the Lord (43:1-12)
Regulations for the Temple Service (43:13—46:24)
Healing Waters (47:1-12)
Division of the Restored Land (47:13—48:35)

COMMENTARY

PROPHECIES OF DOOM BEFORE THE FALL OF JERUSALEM

Ezekiel 1:1—24:27

Vision and Call (1:1—3:27)

Ezekiel's call to be a prophet of God was preceded by a vision of God's chariot moving where it would across the heavens. The framework of this vision suggests a thunderstorm in the Tigris-Euphrates Valley. This may be discerned in the natural sequence of a dark cloud from the north, lightning, the sound of waters, and finally the appearance of a rainbow.

What the time span is in these chapters is hard to determine, but it would appear to be brief. Basically this introductory part of the book consists of a vision and a call in Mesopotamia rather than a series of calls in various places at different times (see Introduction).

Introduction (1:1-3)

The two dates in the superscription refer to two different events. As has been pointed out in the Introduction, the date of Jehoiachin's accession to the throne and the date for the beginning of the Exile is the same year, 598 B.C. Hence, by dating from the beginning of captivity, the exiles were able secretly to date according to the regnal years of King Jehoiachin. The "fifth year" of the Captivity when Ezekiel had his inaugural vision at Tel-abib by the River Chebar would be 593 B.C. These two places have been discovered in upper Mesopotamia where, according to established tradition, Ezekiel lived, thus demonstrating the accuracy of geographical detail in the prophetic work.

The enigmatic "thirtieth year" is also the thirtieth year of the Exile, hence the thirtieth year of Jehoiachin's reign. Through recent archaeological study the fact has been established that Jehoiachin lived and reared a family in captivity. Zedekiah, who succeeded Jehoiachin on the throne of Judah in 597 B.C., was apparently never accepted as the legitimate king by his own subjects and hence his reign was not used for dating. In any case, "the thirtieth year" is a second superscription referring to the occasion when the prophet gathered his prophecies together as a record of God's dealings with men. The record was designed to exonerate the Lord and to help the Chosen People, at least a remnant of them, to understand better the heritage they possessed and the mission which they had been given.

Vision (1:4-28)

A detailed discussion of the vision is not necessary or vital to the understanding of its meaning. Central to the thought are a heavenly chariot, living creatures, and a life-giving Spirit. The chariot is the mobile throne of God, which could move in any and all directions and could go wherever it would. The wheels are full of eyes, which symbolize God's all-seeing power in the world. In these forms the prophet proclaimed that the God of Israel, who had been thought to occupy a stationary throne in the Temple and who by popular conception had been limited to the land of Palestine, was sovereign and omniscient in any place. The living God who meets man in history cannot be limited by historical circumstances—a lesson which needs repeated emphasis.

The living creatures who have four faces are the functional equivalent of the cherubim who supported the Ark of the Covenant in the Holy of Holies (1:5-14). Their four faces—those of a man, an ox, an eagle, and a lion—represent the major areas of created life. Man is God's ultimate creation commissioned to subdue the earth; the lion is the king of wild beasts; the ox is the strongest of domesticated animals; and the eagle rules the air. The chariot was borne aloft above the totality of creation, a symbol of the fact that nature is under the dominion of the Lord.

The figure of God seated on a great sapphire throne is part of the rainbow motif which was afterward frequently used as a model for divine visions in Christian and Jewish writing. Note, however, that the prophet did not look upon the face of God (vss. 26-28).

In the context of the Exile, this was a crucial vision, perhaps a turning point in the drama of Hebrew faith. People uprooted from their homes, who had seen their homeland pillaged and the Temple destroyed, who had themselves been taken captive, might well wonder if God himself had not been destroyed. This vision gave historical and spiritual perspective to the Chosen People. God still rode upon his chariot where and when he willed. He ruled in all creation, both in and above history, and beheld the works of men wherever they were. The God of Ezekiel is the God of all life and history. In any time of great historic change there is always a temptation to believe that God has been caught up in or destroyed by the change itself. This danger is ever present when men do not really accept God as in control of history, but rather see him as controlled by events.

Call from God (2:1—3:3)

Ezekiel falls prostrate before the glory of the Lord (1:28), only to hear a stern divine command to stand up. The term "son of man," as employed here (2:1) and throughout the book, does not have the same meaning as it does in the Book of Daniel or in the apocryphal Book of Enoch. It is certainly not the origin of the term as Jesus used it. "Son of man" as employed in this prophetic work means "man" or "human being," in contrast to God. Ezekiel is given a commission to "the people of Israel," who are variously described as stubborn and rebellious (vs. 4). No successful mission is promised to the prophet. Nevertheless, he is not to be discouraged by the people's words or their looks, although they will be like briers, thorns, and scorpions.

Verse 7 is difficult to understand. The mission of the prophet was not to make his audience hear or believe; his mission was to be the medium of God's word. Success or failure was left entirely to God. This fact puts in bold relief the firm faith of an ancient prophet who considered God, not man, history's chief actor. The prophet's primary task was to proclaim the message, not to get results. It is always so with God's spokesmen. They must realize that the ultimate outcome of a prophetic mission depends not on prophetic skill but upon God's Spirit and will.

Verses 2:8—3:3 depict in a dramatic act the substance of what has previously been given verbally. The prophet is given a scroll on which the content of God's message has been inscribed, and he is told to eat it. On it were written "words of lamentation and mourning and woe." Ezekiel obediently consumed the message of God so that it became part of him. Upon completing the strange meal the prophet comments, "It was in my mouth as sweet as honey" (vs. 3). By word and symbol Ezekiel was commissioned to be God's spokesman to a rebellious house, which included both those people of Judah living in Palestine and those already in exile at Tel-abib.

Detailed Instructions (3:4-27)

The prophet is reminded again that he is sent to his own people and not to a people "of foreign speech and a hard language." Even though there is no language barrier, there will be the barrier of willful rebellion because they have "a hard forehead" and "a stubborn heart." Again Ezekiel is promised that God will make him equal to the task: "Like adamant harder than flint have I made your forehead." He is told first to accept the message in his heart and to hear it with his ears. There is in this oracle the plain requirement that the message is to take possession of the messenger before he delivers it to others. Still no success in mission is promised (vs. 11).

Verses 12-13 indicate that the original vision of God is still a present reality for the prophet. For the first time in the book the prophet is transported by God from place to place (vss. 14-15). This is to be understood as having taken place in a vision. In this case he went "in bitterness" to the exiles at Tel-abib and was "overwhelmed" for seven days among them. The prophetic reaction was one of horror at the commission he had been given (compare Isa. 6). But now, after vision and call, he is among the exiles where his work is to be carried out.

Ezekiel is called to become a watchman for his people (vss. 16-21). The substance of this passage is plain. When the watchman-prophet gives a warning for the People of God, he is relieved of all responsibility for their judgment. But if he fails to warn his people, their blood is on his conscience and he is held responsible. If repentance comes, the prophet is the instrument of salvation. Thus the joint responsibility and privilege of the prophetic office are spelled out.

The prophet who has returned from "the plain," where he had seen the glory of the Lord, to dwell among the exiles at Tel-abib, is told to go back to "the plain" for further instruction. There, overwhelmed, he falls to the ground, but the Spirit sets him upon his feet. He is instructed to shut himself in his house where cords will be placed upon him, where he will be bound and become dumb (vss. 24-26). "But when I speak with you, I will open your mouth," promises the Lord (vs. 27). This strange experience has been explained in many ways. Some believe that Ezekiel was literally imprisoned and that he was actually dumb, perhaps like the father of John the Baptist. Others understand the occurrence as pure symbolism or vision. It would seem to be explained best in the following manner: Ezekiel played the *role* of a prisoner in order to underscore his message concerning Jerusalem; moreover, it was only when he spoke on behalf of God that he spoke at all in public.

Visions and Oracles of Judgment (4:1—7:27)

In this general division of the book chapters 4 and 5 deal with five dramatic acts of the prophet which describe in various ways the siege and the exile to follow. The reader should remember that the Hebrew prophets proclaimed the word of God through action as well as through word. For example, Isaiah walked naked through the streets to dramatize the fact that Egypt and Ethiopia would be captured by Assyrian power (Isa. 20:1-2). Jeremiah broke a pottery jar as a symbol of God's intent with respect to Judah (Jer. 19), and when Hananiah broke the yoke of wood, a yoke of iron indicated the Captivity which would become unbreakable (Jer. 27:1—28:16). The Book of Ezekiel swarms with dramatic acts such as the eating of a scroll (2:8—3:3), the dramatizing of captivity (5:1-4), the portraying of the siege of Jerusalem (4:1-3). There are numerous other instances where the prophet's act contains a message beyond the power of words to express (for example, ch. 12). It should be understood that the true prophet's word or deed was really God's word or deed, creating the event forecast.

Symbolic Siege of the City (4:1-17)

The prophet is instructed to take a mud brick and draw a map of Jerusalem on it. Such mud brick maps were common in Mesopotamia. Pretending that the map is the city, Ezekiel then carries out a miniature siege of Jerusalem. The prophet, taking the role of God, sets up camps and battering rams, and an iron plate is placed between him and the city. This prophetic act is "a sign for the house of Israel."

Following the siege there is another fascinating demonstration. Ezekiel is instructed to lie three hundred and ninety days on one side as an indication of the length of Israel's captivity. He lies on his left side for Israel because a person who stood facing east in Palestine, and then lay back on his left side, would be looking northward where Israel was located. The face would be southward to Judah when he lay on his right side. The number of days

26   EZEKIEL 5:1-17

has been a source of difficulty. Actually it is better to understand one hundred and ninety days, as does the Greek translation. Approximately one hundred and ninety years elapsed between the beginning of Israel's captivity, sometime after 734 B.C., and the beginning of return in 538 B.C. (vs. 5).

Ezekiel is not only to lie upon his side for this extended period during the siege, but he must also bare his arm while, as God's representative, he faces the city (a map on a mud brick). In this manner the prophet demonstrates that God is the chief adversary of Judah. The prophet remains bound during the siege. In all probability this symbolic act was repeated daily, but whether the full cycle of 190 days was completed cannot be said.

Details of life under siege are given in verses 9-17. Scarcity of food and water is described; barley cakes are to be baked with human excrement as fuel, and there is the forecast that "Thus shall the people of Israel eat their bread unclean, among the nations whither I will drive them" (vs. 13). After his natural revulsion the prophet receives the concession from God that animal manure may become fuel for cooking. Hunger and thirst under siege are the terrors which shall cause the people to "waste away under their punishment" (vs. 17).

Extent of the Desolation (5:1-17)

A shaved head was a mark of captivity, so the prophet is told to shave off his hair in public and to dispose of it in three ways. One third is to be burned with fire in the midst of the city. One third is to be struck by the sword "round about the city." The remaining one third is to be scattered to the wind. A small part of this portion is to be bound in the prophet's robe (vs. 3), but even some of these hairs are to be burned.

Following this prophetic act there is an interlude wherein justification for God's judgment is clearly and forcefully presented. Judah has "rebelled" against God's ordinances and statutes even more than the nations round about (vs. 6). Because this is so, destruction is necessary. In verse 10 and following, the horrors of siege are described and the three phases of destruction are interpreted. Cannibalism often occurred under the conditions of siege (vs. 10). The people who have defiled God's sanctuary are to be destroyed: one part by pestilence and famine, one part by the sword, and one part by dispersion to the ends of the earth.

Verses 13-17 introduce a dominant theme of Ezekiel's prophecy. God's actions in history, whether for judgment or for redemption, are all designed that the nations may know that he is the Lord, the only God, and that they may see his true nature. Judah in captivity will be "a warning and a horror" to the nations. Destruction by war and famine must be understood as God's manifestation of his true character. His purpose in the Covenant was to reveal himself to all nations through his servant people. But Israel and Judah failed to co-operate with the divine will. Because of their disobedience he will use their failure to manifest to all men his integrity and justice. If God cannot be revealed through an obedient Israel, he will reveal himself in judgment on a rebellious people.

Idolatry Condemned (6:1-14)

Addressing the mountains and hills of Israel, the ravines and the valleys, where idolatry was practiced, Ezekiel promises that the sword will come against the "high places," where idolatry was in vogue. Altars of sacrifice and of incense will be broken, and sacred areas will be desecrated by the presence of dead bodies. Thus idolatry, like every other phase of the corrupt life of Judah, will be wiped out and the idolaters destroyed.

At this point (vs. 8) the prophet changes pace and speaks to those who will escape the sword. Verses 8-10 were probably added later, but certainly they belong to the thought pattern of Ezekiel. The theme is that people broken for their sin and sent into captivity will "remember [God] among the nations." "They will be loathsome in their own sight for the evils which they have committed, for all their abominations." Under these circumstances the dispersed people, repentant for their past, will be a witness to God.

Verses 11-12 are a separate ecstatic song, phrased in the original as a kind of dance form. After this rhythmic piece the subject of idolatry on every high hill and under every green tree, a sure reference to a type of nature worship (Baal worship), is resumed (vs. 13). The final verse sums up the resultant judgment on Judah's idolatry.

Punishment for National Sin (7:1-27)

The Day of the Lord, when God will enter victoriously into history, is viewed in the perspective which Amos had earlier given to it. God's day for Judah was not to be a day of redemption but a time of judgment upon national sin. There was doubtless still a widespread popular misconception that God's day of victory would be a joyous time for Judah. But since Judah had not accepted the Covenant love of God, God's coming was necessarily to be a visitation of judgment (vss. 1-4). God will come as an enemy because his people have turned against him. Divine judgment will come in the destruction of this rebellious people.

The section includes a poetic announcement that the Day of the Lord has come. The proclamation is made in staccato tones (vs. 10). The ultimate consequences of national character have come to full bloom. Violent strength and the power of wealth are useless. Among people in siege or captivity, there is no pre-eminence (vs. 11). There is no normal trade among captives, because "none can maintain his life." The only real support for life is God's blessing; this Judah has lost.

When the attack came there was no resistance, no determination to defend homeland or heritage. "None goes to battle" (vs. 14). Famine, sword, and pestilence together do a thorough job of destruction. For clothes men have sackcloth, and their heads are shaved by their captors (vs. 18). Money is useless because there is nothing to buy; since it cannot deliver the city from doom, it is cast out as an "unclean thing" (vs. 19). All the precious things which Judah proudly possesses will prove under these circumstances to be worthless. Desolation will be complete. The land will be prey to foreigners and the wicked will possess it. The Temple will be sacked and profaned, because it has been misused for idolatry and other false religious practices (vs. 22).

Bloody crimes of violence give God cause to "bring the worst of the nations" to take possession of the land. Thus the Almighty "will put an end to their proud might, and their holy places shall be profaned" (vs. 24). Notice that it is not *God's* holy place but *their* "holy places." The prophet understands that God has removed himself, or will remove himself, from the Temple environs.

Ordinary sources of strength in any society break down under pressure in Judah, and there is no reason for hope. Prophetic vision, priestly interpretation, elders' advice, and royal leadership all fail. The king mourns and the people of the land tremble as if with palsy. Judgment is sure, but through it God will make them know who he is and what his purpose is.

Visions of the Prophet (8:1—11:25)

Abominations Seen in Jerusalem (8:1-18)

The setting is Tel-abib in the house of Ezekiel, where he is surrounded by the "elders of Judah," perhaps personal advisers to the prophet. God's glorious presence, in a form like that of the vision in chapter 1, is sensed, and "the form of a hand" takes the prophet by a lock of his head, lifting him up "between heaven and earth." This is patently a vision, not physical transport of the prophet, who himself explains that the hand "brought me in visions of God to Jerusalem."

Ezekiel is directed to lift up his eyes and look "in the direction of the north" where a pagan god named Baal-Hadad was traditionally thought to dwell. He sees the "image of jealousy," some kind of Baal image. God speaks to his prophet about "the great abominations that the house of Israel are committing," which in effect drive God far from his sanctuary. Since such worship is carried on in the environs of God's house, the Temple can no longer be the dwelling place of God. Once he has removed his presence from the Temple, there is no power to prevent its destruction. With tragic accent the prophet is told, "But you will see still greater abominations."

An underground secret room is discovered by the prophet who, after digging through a wall, comes to a door. The prophet must not be required to be completely consistent or logical when he supplies details such as "a door" and "a hole." His meaning is quite clear, namely, that he uncovered the secret chamber where the elders were worshiping. The walls were covered with pictures of creeping things and unclean animals, reminiscent of magical paintings in Egypt and probably also representing Chaldean influence. This frescoed room was the setting for "all the idols of the house of Israel" (vs. 10). Seventy elders of the house of Israel, including Ja-azaniah, stood before these pictures and idols, each with a censer in his hand, burning incense to false deities.

Doubtless these elders were still publicly loyal to God but their actual worship was dedicated to images in this secret place. Every man was worshiping in his "room of pictures" because he felt "The LORD does not see . . . the LORD has forsaken the land." This is the key to spiritual decline within the city and is the problem with which most of Ezekiel's early prophetic activity had to do. Men felt that God had forsaken them and that they were free to turn to other gods; yet there was the strange inconsistency of their playing both ends against the middle. Pretense of being true to a great heritage was a cover for their actual loyalty.

Not only were the seventy elders in the grip of a new idolatry, but also there were women weeping for Tammuz (vs. 14). This Babylonian god was the husband or lover of the goddess Ishtar and was himself the god of vegetation. When vegetation withered and died in summer heat, women would weep for their dead god. Along with this aspect of the fertility cult went other debasements and orgies. In this kind of atmosphere how could God continue to be present in the city?

At the inner court of the Temple, somewhere "between the porch and the altar," twenty-five men sat with their backs to the Temple "and their faces toward the east, worshiping the sun toward the east." Ordinarily the Jew faced the Temple when he worshiped, but these worshipers turned their backs to the Temple and their faces toward the sun. In addition to the mention of this act of nature worship, another cryptic reference to some nature cult is made in the words, "Lo, they put the branch to their nose" (vs. 17). Because Jerusalem was thus saturated with worship of Baal images, Tammuz, and the sun, God would deal with the city in wrath and would not spare (vs. 18).

Vision of Utter Destruction (9:1-11)

In the midst of his visionary review of the situation in Jerusalem the prophet sees in all its horrible detail the final destruction of the city. Usually he defines destruction as ordained of God to be carried out in the regular processes of history, but not in this case. For the first time in biblical literature there is a well-developed apocalyptic (superhistorical) description of God's judgment. This sort of description becomes quite common later in Zechariah and Daniel as well as in some Intertestament books (for example, Enoch) and in the New Testament Book of Revelation. The prophet hears God command, "Draw near, you executioners of the city, each with his destroying weapon in his hand" (vs. 1). Six men appear carrying weapons for slaughter, and with them there is another man, dressed in linen and having a writing case at his side. These are the emissaries of God and may in fact be the prototypes of the seven angels of God who later became prominent in Jewish and Christian writing. The man in linen is dressed

like a priest, but the significance of that fact escapes us at this
late date. These seven sinister figures go and stand by the bronze
altar.

Significantly we are told that "the glory of the God of Israel"
had gone up from the cherubim where it traditionally rested and
had paused on the threshold (vs. 3). From that point the Lord in-
structs the man in linen to put a mark upon the foreheads of the
men who sigh and groan over all the abominations that are committed in Jerusalem (vs. 4). Thus the man in linen is *de facto* the
priest or scribe of God. Those who do not show signs of remorse
over the low spiritual state of life are to be utterly destroyed. Nobody, either young or old, is to be spared except those who have
a special mark on their foreheads.

Destruction must start where guilt has its deepest root (vs. 6).
The sanctuary had been a front for everything except its intended
purposes. Here pretense and delusion had flourished. For these
reasons destruction began, according to the divine directive, with
the elders who stood before the sanctuary, who were themselves
deeply implicated in national and social guilt. Having been used
for shame, the house that had been dedicated to the glory of God
is now defiled and destroyed by the Lord's command.

Orders are carried out. When the prophet in sheer agony of
spirit asks the natural question, "Wilt thou destroy all that remains
of Israel in the outpouring of thy wrath upon Jerusalem?", the
Lord recites the record of "the land . . . full of blood" whose leaders say, "The LORD has forsaken the land, and the LORD does not
see" (vs. 9). The man dressed in linen reports with finality to the
Lord, "I have done as thou didst command me." Thus, in apocalyptic style, the prophet portrays God's final judgment upon a
land which openly pledged loyalty to him but secretly worshiped
other gods.

Renewal of the Vision of God (10:1-22)

Chapter 10 is a conglomerate which in all probability must be
credited to an editor, although its content is substantially the same
as that of chapter 1. The apocalyptic figure of destruction dressed
in linen (ch. 9) is now related to the God whose presence has been
seen in the plain in Mesopotamia. Already the unmarked citizens
of the city are dead; now the city itself must be destroyed. To ob-
tain the destructive fire of God the man in linen is ordered to get
coals from among the wheels and scatter them over the city. Once

this connection is made, a descriptive paragraph follows which locates the glory of the Lord and follows the movement thereof. It has moved from the cherubim to the threshold of the house, the attendant noise being heard as far out as the outer court. God is preparing to leave the sanctuary which is no longer worthy to be his dwelling place (vss. 3-5). Following this, the order for destruction is given, and it is carried out by the man in linen.

Verses 9-17 are a shorter description of the inaugural vision of the prophet. It is quite possible that the vision was actually renewed in the prophet's experience at this time, but the description of the vision is, as we would expect, patterned after the literary material in chapter 1 mixed with apocalyptic elements.

Verses 18-19 reveal the major purpose or theme of the chapter, namely, the withdrawal of God's presence from his traditional dwelling place. Reasons for this have been detailed in the previous chapters; now only the act itself remains to be carried out. The cherubim, over whom the divine presence (Shekinah) stood, rose from the Holy of Holies and came to the East Gate of the Temple. There at the gate where the cherubim were poised, the glory of the Lord was seen, rather than in the Holy of Holies where it had long been housed.

Verses 20-22 identify this vision with the prophet's inaugural vision seen by the River Chebar. Descriptive details are given as evidence that this "glory of the LORD" about to depart from the Temple is the same glory as that which was seen by the prophet in Mesopotamia.

Denunciation and Hope (11:1-25)

After the vision of destruction and the withdrawal of God's glory, the prophet returns in vision to visit in Jerusalem (vs. 1). This is not to be taken as a continuation of the same visionary experience depicted in chapter 8 but must be understood as another occasion, grouped here with earlier material because of similarity of content.

Twenty-five men (not to be identified with the sun worshipers in chapter 8), including one Ja-azaniah (not the same as in 8:11) and Pelatiah, princes of the city, were talking among themselves about the future and were saying, "The time is not near to build houses; this city is the caldron, and we are the flesh." Their conversation reflected the hopeless pessimism which gripped the city. God orders the prophet to explain that it is those who have already been slain by the injustices of an unrighteous society who are the flesh in the city which is a caldron. But the guilty ones who still remain in the city God will bring forth and "will judge . . . at the border of Israel." Thus the explanation is completed, "This city shall not be your caldron, nor shall you be the flesh in the midst of it; I will judge you at the border of Israel" (vs. 11). This is possibly a reference to King Zedekiah and his entourage who were captured while seeking to escape to Riblah. The old refrain is then caught up again as the divine voice explains why such harsh judgment must fall on this people (vs. 12).

The incident of the death of Pelatiah (vs. 13) is one of the knottiest historical problems which the student of Ezekiel must face. While Ezekiel, still physically in Tel-abib, was making his prophecy to a company of men who were in Palestine, one of their number, Pelatiah, dropped dead. It is obvious from the prophet's emotional reaction to the incident that he felt responsible for the death of Pelatiah. It appears that his word caused the unexpected demise. On this basis many interpreters have assigned Ezekiel to a Palestinian locale. Two things may be said. First, the prophecy as we have it was written toward the end of Ezekiel's career and part of it was written after his death. It tends therefore to link cause and effect that were not originally connected. This was possibly the case with the Pelatiah incident. Second, it can be logically asked whether Pelatiah was actually in Palestine or in Tel-abib when he died suddenly. In the light of the prophet's mixture of visionary experience with normal life, it is difficult to know where Pelatiah was. If he were a leader of the exiles, his death as a result of the impact of the prophecy would be unusual but understandable. In any case the death of Pelatiah was a foretaste of the much darker tragedy which was about to occur on history's stage, the fall of Jerusalem.

The prophet now turns his attention from the people of Jerusalem to his "fellow exiles," in order to interpret their lot in the light of God's activity (vss. 14-21). To them he offers a promise. The ones remaining in Palestine are saying of the exiles, "They have gone far from the LORD; to us this land is given for a possession." Jeremiah faced the same issue with audiences in Jerusalem (Jer. 24 and 29). The Lord through his prophet explains that though he has brought some into exile away from the sanctuary, yet he has been "a sanctuary to them for a while" in the lands of their exile (vs. 16).

The Lord now promises that his people will return from exile and that restoration of the land will follow. Moreover, since a fundamental change in human nature is required before the future can be bright with hope, God declares that he will give to his people "a new heart, and . . . a new spirit" (vss. 19, margin). The very essence of man's being will be altered drastically by God, so that the Covenant relationship, reaching back in its origin to the Mosaic era, will be restored to its original terms: "They shall be my people, and I will be their God." But even in the brighter future those who do not have a new heart and a new spirit have no such hope.

This beautiful section doubtless belongs to Ezekiel but may have been put into its present literary setting after the fall of Jerusalem, when the various oracles were being collected. In the light of subsequent history and from the point of view of theology it belongs here, even though chronologically its composition must be placed later than the first part of the chapter.

The throne of God upon which his glory has dwelt is now removed from the midst of the city (vss. 22-25). The breach of Covenant by the people has caused God to withdraw his presence. This time "the glory of the LORD" went beyond the Temple environs to the mountains on the east side of the city, and there stopped as if to watch the destruction to follow. Verse 24 implies clearly that the Spirit, who had brought Ezekiel in vision to Jerusalem in the first instance, now returned him to the exiles in Chaldea.

Some interpreters hold that Ezekiel's message was irrelevant for those living at Tel-abib, but this is surely not the case, as verse 25 indicates. In Tel-abib false hopes of a quick return were still treasured and Jerusalem was the visible symbol for undying optimism. Part of the prophetic task was to destroy false optimism by proclaiming that God's abode was no longer in Jerusalem and that the city was doomed.

Prophecies Against Jerusalem (12:1—19:14)

Captivity Predicted (12:1-20)

It is typical of Ezekiel that an action speaks louder than a word. The dramatic act described in this chapter symbolizes the fact that the people and their king will seek to escape from the land before its capture by an invader. Following the prophetic act Ezekiel describes the horrors of life in exile.

The people to whom Ezekiel was sent were from the outset called "a rebellious house." On this occasion the deserved appellation is given to them once more. Because they are rebels the prophet is instructed to go through the motions of preparing baggage for exile. Bag and baggage were to be openly displayed in the sight of the people of Tel-abib, who had already experienced flight and exile, so that they might understand what was about to happen to Jerusalem. The baggage was to be made ready in the day, but escape would begin at evening. Thus there would be protection from the sun and also escape from detection by Chaldean guards along the way.

Ezekiel was instructed to prepare his baggage, then when evening came he was to dig a hole in the wall to indicate an escape in secret (vs. 5). The wall through which he was to dig was doubtless made of mud brick, a common building material in Mesopotamia. He was to carry his baggage in the darkness and to cover his face, "that you may not see the land." Thus he was to act as a sign or message to the house of Israel.

The prophetic act is in verses 8-20 specifically applied to the fate of Zedekiah, who actually was king but who is always called "prince" (vs. 10) by Ezekiel, probably because the prophet considered Jehoiachin the rightful ruler. When curious people asked the prophet for an explanation of his eccentric behavior, he was to give this answer: "This oracle concerns the prince in Jerusalem and all the house of Israel who are in it." Ezekiel was a sign of the coming captivity and exile of the inhabitants of Jerusalem.

Zedekiah is the one who "shall lift his baggage upon his shoulder in the dark, and shall go forth; he shall dig through the wall and go out through it; he shall cover his face, that he may not see the land with his eyes" (vs. 12). The historical record of Zedekiah's flight from Jerusalem is preserved in II Kings 25:4-7; Jeremiah 39:4-8; 52:7-11. When the armies of Nebuchadnezzar finally breached the city wall, Zedekiah escaped by a secret gate in his garden. However, he was captured by the Chaldeans at a place on the border called Riblah. Verse 13 predicts the horrible fate which will befall the king. According to the historical records it was the fate of the ill-starred monarch to see his sons slain and then to be blinded. He was brought bound to Babylon, where he was imprisoned "till the day of his death" (see Jer. 52:10-11).

At this point in the prophecy God renews his threat to scatter and to destroy Israel, leaving but a few to survive so that they may confess their failure among the nations and by confession justify the divine judgment upon Jerusalem (Ezek. 12:14-16). Verses 17-20 are in essence a repetition of the description of life under siege as given in 4:16. Not only the city but the entire land will be laid waste, and Palestine will be a desolation.

Popular Proverbs (12:21-28)

No better index to popular thought and the real temper of spirit among a people can be found than the proverbs heard in the streets. What were people saying in the time of Ezekiel? They were saying, "The days grow long, and every vision comes to naught" (vs. 22b). This proverb caused God to command his prophet to announce that there would be no more delay, but that every prophetic vision was about to be fulfilled (vss. 23-25).

People were also using another proverb which spoke of judgment as far distant: "The vision that he sees is for many days hence, and he prophesies of times far off" (vs. 27). To this the Lord replies through his prophet, again warning of imminent judgment (vs. 28).

The popular idea was that a "vision" was a meaningless, imaginative experience of the prophet, which, though frightening, would never come to fruition. But even if it were a true forecast, it was directed to the distant future and had no relevance in the present situation. Prophets had been famous for denunciation and prediction of doom, but obviously their predictions had not yet been fulfilled. Thus have people in all times sought to make faith irrelevant to life, either depicting faith as an empty claim or pushing its demands into the far future. The primary design in such efforts is to remove it from the present where it makes a claim upon man's life and speaks to his quality of living.

False Prophets Described and Judged (13:1-16)

This well-known passage is an analysis in depth of the prophetic failure in Judah's time of distress. Ezekiel is ordered by God to speak against the prophets of Israel for three reasons: (1) They prophesied out of their own minds and followed their own spirit; (2) in Israel's distress they did not stand; and (3) they deliberately lied and then expected God to fulfill their words.

A genuine prophet spoke on behalf of another and not in his own right; he was a medium for God's word, not for man's wisdom. False prophets spoke what came to their minds at the moment and followed the inclinations of their own hearts. Yet, for this human wisdom they claimed the authority of "Thus saith the LORD." They had "seen nothing," yet they proclaimed much. These men were as useless as "foxes among ruins." They had not "gone up into the breaches, or built up a wall for the house of Israel." In other words, they fulfilled no function in a crisis. Actually the reference to the wall describes the spiritual vitality of the people, which was part of the prophetic responsibility. Later the Pharisees spoke of the "fence of the law" which protected them against mundane intrusions. The wall of spiritual defense had not been built by the prophets, hence they are adjudged false prophets.

The initiative which must always be reserved for God is taken by the prophets. Instead of receiving the word from God which he then will perform, they speak their own word and expect him to fulfill it lest failure should embarrass his standing. A rhetorical question sums up and closes the paragraph.

On account of their delusive visions and blasphemous attitudes the Lord is against the prophets. Judgment is spelled out in three categories: "They shall not be in the council of my people, nor be enrolled in the register of the house of Israel, nor shall they enter the land of Israel" (vs. 9b). To put it simply, they are disinherited because they have been unworthy of their true heritage. Their message has been what people wanted to hear: "Peace." But the problem was, ". . . there is no peace," because the prophets and people had not done those things which make for peace. The word "peace" stands for that condition of balance and happiness in life which proceeds out of the Covenant relationship with God. Peace, as most students of the Bible know, refers not so much to absence of conflict as to completeness of life. That kind of fulfillment can be had only through harmonious relationship with Almighty God, a relationship which was woefully absent in Judah's corporate life.

The pretense of religious strength and security typified by these prophets is magnificently described in the figure of a crumbling wall which is about to fall. Instead of repairing it properly, "these prophets daub it with whitewash" (vs. 10). When the storm comes the "whitewash" (pretense) will be washed off and the wall will tumble in rubble to the ground. The wall is identified with the prophets who will themselves be destroyed in the destruction of their own handiwork (vss. 14-16). The last sentence of the paragraph has a genuine finality about it. Thus the shallow optimism which when nothing was right loudly proclaimed that all was well, was utterly liquidated, together with its purveyors.

Prophetesses Doomed (13:17-23)

When true religion does not fulfill its assigned role properly, substitutes for it begin to appear in numerous places and countless forms. The women described in verses 17-23, obviously soothsayers, witches, or sorceresses, are good examples of such perverse substitutes for religion. We should not be surprised that this type of activity was found alongside the high religion of Israel; even church people today are fascinated by such expressions of the occult as crystal-ball and horoscope readings. The exact meaning of verse 18 escapes us. It is probable that the "bands" were symbols of the power with which these sorceresses made people their captives. We do not know what kind of practice may be described in the words "and make veils . . . in the hunt for souls." That the main purpose of these witches was to make a profit is stated plainly and unmistakably. "For handfuls of barley and for pieces of bread" these misguided and evil women sought to influence God's people in matters of life and death (vs. 19).

For these reasons God condemns the deceit of sorcery and the sorceresses. He will destroy the badges of their art ("magic bands") and will let the souls that they have hunted "go free like birds." It is possible that such women claimed a power over the dead as well as over the living. The effect of such a claim would be to dishearten the righteous and to encourage the wicked (vs. 22). It is always so with the magical rites of false religion which have no relation to moral values.

The Elders of Israel (14:1-11)

The elders of Israel met with the prophet, apparently in Tel-abib, but the intent of the message which resulted was for the inhabitants of both Tel-abib and Jerusalem. Ezekiel, as we have previously pointed out, considered Judah one people irrespective of their geographical locale. Idolatry, which has already been denounced by the prophet in chapter 6 and specifically faced by him in chapter 8, is now clearly shown as sin against the Lord.

The elders are described as men who have "taken their idols into their hearts, and set the stumbling block of their iniquity before their faces" (vs. 3). The reference is to passionate and complete attachment to idols. Having possessed the heart of man, the physical object or "stumbling block" is set before his face. The deep contempt in which the prophet held idols is manifest in his word for "idols" (literally, "rolls of dung") used thirty-nine times in the book.

Often in the Old Testament, God is depicted as jealous. Against this backdrop we are to understand the words "that I may lay hold of the hearts of the house of Israel, who are all estranged from me, through their idols." It cannot be said whether or not this means that the prophet understood that God would get at the *cause* of idolatry, which is in the heart; but it is true that idolatry reaches far deeper than its overt and meaningless expression.

"Repent and turn away" is the exhortation of the prophet to Israel (vs. 6). The Hebrew term for "repent" simply means "turn" or "return" or "turn away." To the Hebrew mind, the idea of repentance was to "turn away from," that is, to "do an about-face." That is what the prophet urged his hearers to do: to turn away from their idols.

The hypocrisy of a religion which still seeks a word from the Lord through prophets while continuing to worship idols is set in bold relief by Ezekiel. He says that neither Israelite nor sojourner can do this without facing divine rebuff and rebuke. Furthermore, when such spiritual schizophrenics come to the prophet, he must not speak God's word to them. One must remember that to the Hebrew the word of God was not just a sound with meaning, it was creative power. If a prophet gives the word of God to a man who follows any religion but is loyal to none, the prophet as well as the inquirer is under God's judgment.

The punishment of spiritual duplicity is carried out in order that Israel "may go no more astray" from God. The enticements of syncretism are dangers which every generation must face, yet they are so subtle that they are hard to resist. God will destroy the purveyors of distorted religion in order that his Covenant with Israel may be re-established. The terms of that Covenant—"that they may be my people and I may be their God"—provide a fitting close for a passage which has described with horror how the Covenant has been forgotten, ignored, and destroyed by all elements in society.

Present Doom and Future Hope (14:12-23)

This section should be understood as a recurrence of a basic theme which the writer and editors never let the reader forget: Present doom is a prelude to future renewal, through a remnant of purified and obedient Israel. God renews his warning of judgment by famine and exile because the land has been "acting faithlessly" (vs. 12). The inevitability of destruction is demonstrated when the prophet, in terms that are reminiscent of the story of Sodom and Gomorrah, says that even if Noah, Daniel, and Job were living in this land, all their righteousness could not stay the hand of God's judgment. In the case of Sodom and Gomorrah (Gen. 18:16-33), Abraham was promised that the presence of faithful folk in the cities would turn the wrath of God. No such promise is made to Jerusalem, whose sin is more heinous than that of Sodom and Gomorrah. The presence of righteous men, whose place in history was established on the basis of their righteous life, would not be enough to stop judgment.

A word about these figures from the past should suffice. Noah is well known from the story of the Flood, while the Book of Job preserves a very ancient story of uprightness. Together with these two super-saints a certain "Dan'el," not to be identified with the main character of the Book of Daniel, is also listed. It seems improbable that a contemporary would be listed in the same breath with the most ancient sages. The name "Dan'el" appears in an ancient Canaanite source and it reappears in the apocryphal Book of Enoch. In both cases this "Dan'el," dating from early times, is represented as a righteous and good man from among the most ancient sages. Of these three the prophet speaks with an air of finality, "Even if Noah, Daniel, and Job were in it . . . they would deliver but their own lives" (vs. 20).

The second paragraph of the section sounds again the recurrent theme of destruction by sword, famine, wild beasts, and pestilence. When any survivors from this holocaust are brought forth, they will demonstrate the necessity and justice of God's destructive judgment. The message is directed to the exiles in Tel-abib, who are asking most urgently why God would destroy free Jerusalem. But when the exiles witness the destruction and meet the survivors they will be consoled (vs. 23). Once more the aim of God's righteous judgment is stressed; it is that the remnant may still trust him and desire to be his people. He is not capricious; he is One whose offer of life when accepted is truly life but when rejected is destruction.

Israel a Useless Vine (15:1-8)

This chapter is built around an ancient allegory of the vine, which is useless for purposes other than producing fruit. The original core of the oracle is to be found in verses 2-5; the remainder serves as expansion and application to the current situation in life.

The prophecy begins with a rhetorical question expecting a negative answer: "Is wood taken from it to make anything?" Obviously the wood of the vine is greatly inferior to any other kind of wood. The next questions are satirical and also require negative replies. A peg cannot be made of it; it does not burn evenly in the fire; when it is whole it is used for nothing; after it has been charred in fire it is even more worthless. Taking his cue from the word "fire," the prophet applies this ancient oracle, which was probably well known among his hearers, to the contemporary situation. Jerusalem will become like "wood of the vine" for fuel. Even though some will escape from the fire "charred" but not consumed, eventually the fire will consume even them. We should understand this chapter as another figure employed to reinforce the main theme of the prophet; that is, Israel has reached the point where neither redemption nor rescue is possible.

Parable of an Unfaithful Wife (16:1-63)

This chapter, like several others, is based on a parable which is applied to the life of Israel. Like all parables, this one cannot be pressed in every detail; there are inconsistencies. But the main idea illustrated is clear, namely, that Israel is like a wife unfaithful to her covenant position. In this respect the chapter is akin to the Book of Hosea.

Ezekiel calls in question the purity of origin which was the basis for Judah's false national pride when he says: "Your origin and your birth are of the land of the Canaanites; your father was an Amorite, and your mother a Hittite" (vs. 3). Amorites appeared on the stage of history about 2000 B.C. and later gave rise to the reign of Hammurabi in the first dynasty of Babylon. The Assyrian word means "westerner," and in this general sense of the term Abraham was in fact an Amorite; that is, he was part of the great Amorite migration. The historic connection with the Hittites, who were a non-Semitic people, is not so direct. The empire of the Hittites flourished from 1600-1200 B.C. in Asia Minor and encompassed the northern section of Syria in the early fourteenth century B.C. Thus the prophet reminds his people that they have been settled in a land not their own and that neither paternal nor maternal ancestry gives basis for pride.

Having made this general introduction the prophet turns from the international framework to a magnetic and beautiful story. A girl at birth was unwanted by her parents, so without being washed after birth she was exposed on the mountain to die. In ancient times society gave parents the right to leave an unwanted child exposed to the elements until death came. This child, unwanted, was left in a field on the day she was born, and no eye pitied her (vss. 4-5). A stranger (the Lord) passed by, saw the pitiable condition of the child weltering in her blood, and said, "Live, and grow up like a plant of the field." So she grew up to young womanhood in the desert, but she was naked, bare, and unprotected (vss. 6-7).

Later the stranger came back to the wilderness and recognized another crisis in the life of the young woman. This time he plighted his troth to her in "covenant," cleansing her of the blood of uncleanness, covering her with his robe, and making her his wife (vss. 8-9). There can be no doubt that these words refer to God's Covenant with Israel in the wilderness. The waif from the woods, now a full-grown woman, is established in "regal estate," clothed in luxury and secure in plenty. Indeed, she becomes famous for her beauty (vss. 13-14).

Instead of keeping covenant with her betrothed husband, the woman trusted in her beauty and practiced harlotry with every passer-by. She used the gifts bestowed upon her by her husband to buy the attention of her lovers. Verses 16-19 describe in lurid detail the household of the unfaithful wife, where God's gifts are employed for the wrong ends. In her infidelity nothing or no one was spared. The prophet describes the woman as sacrificing her children to the objects of her unholy desire, clearly referring to child sacrifice to the god Molech. Finally, the woman is condemned in words which combine pathos and satire: "And in all your abominations and your harlotries you did not remember the days of your youth, when you were naked and bare, weltering in your blood" (vs. 22).

The prophet's story, the meaning of which is transparently clear, is now applied to Israel's life in the community of nations (vss. 23-43). The message of Isaiah has probably had some influence on the concept here. Apparently infidelity is detected in international affairs, where a political treaty almost always led to syncretism in religion. The Israelites often dealt with the Egyptians and thereby became spiritually unfaithful to the Lord. In this particular reference the age of Solomon is meant. Political marriages and religious syncretism brought Egyptian influence to a high point during Solomon's reign. Following that, harlotry with Assyria is charged. Historically this tendency to live in treaty relationship reached its high-water mark in the age of King Manasseh, whose unlamented death was not long past. The prophet points to the alliance of Judah with Chaldea, which was even then in effect in Jerusalem. God has punished his people, but to no avail, for even pagan nations were shocked at Israel's lewd behavior.

Verses 35-43a detail the judgment of God against the faithless wife, who shall be stripped in shame before her former lovers, who have come to despise her. With stones and swords she will be punished. The place of her adultery will be utterly destroyed, and she will not be allowed to pursue her crimson habits again. Because Israel had forgotten the early days of her history, when God had found her in a wilderness as a child, made a Covenant with her, and in love claimed her for his own, the Lord of history will now execute judgment.

Verse 44 relates the proverb of the faithless wife to another proverb concerning two sisters who compete with each other in their depth of moral disrepute. The proverb, "Like mother, like daughter," goes back to pick up the initial statement of the chapter, which declared that Israel had a Hittite mother and an Amorite father. Samaria is identified as the elder sister in the north and Sodom as the younger sister in the south. Samaria was the capital of Israel, established during the reigns of Omri and Ahab, and is frequently described as sister to Judah. Sodom, the younger sister of Judah, did not actually come from the same background of history or race. It did, however, represent the lowest level to which people had sunk, a city upon which God's fierce judgment came with final destructiveness. Yet the prophet says of Sodom that she had never reached the depths to which Judah has descended (vs. 48).

In order to make his case Ezekiel catalogues the sins of Sodom and of Samaria. Proud Sodom had a surfeit of food, prosperous ease without care for the needy, a haughty spirit, and idolatrous worship (vss. 49-50). Samaria had not done half the sins which Judah committed; yet Samaria had long since been destroyed by the wrath of the Lord. The point in this passage is that Judah has become worse than the worst, hence God's judgment is inevitable (vss. 51-52).

Judgment for the unfaithful, however, does not end with punishment. Restoration for Sodom, Samaria, and Judah is promised (vs. 53). Meanwhile Judah has now become a reproach to her neighbor, the Philistines, and has taken the place of Sodom as the epitome of human wickedness. After promising harsh judgment for Covenant-breaking, the Lord points to the time when the temporary Covenant will be established as an "everlasting covenant" (vs. 60), unaffected by the contingencies of time. In the period of restoration Sodom and Samaria shall become no longer sisters on equal footing but daughters, subject to Jerusalem. The everlasting Covenant and the redemption of God's people must inevitably affect and influence neighboring countries.

When this Covenant is renewed, Jerusalem will know the Lord as the true God; she will remember her past with shame and will be silent. A renewed people will recognize God as the Source of all being, the One who alone is worthy of devotion, and they will know that they have nothing in themselves in which to boast.

Parable of the Two Eagles (17:1-24)

International relations and international religion could not be separated, because vassalage to a foreign political power usually meant homage to a foreign god (see also 16:23-29). The two great empires with which Judah had to deal were Egypt and Chaldea (neo-Babylonia). Seldom in Judah's history had she been more of a pawn on the international chessboard than she was now, with her sovereign rulers being switched at will by one king after another (see Introduction).

The riddle or allegory which is proposed by the prophet is transparent in its meaning and is directed at Jerusalem's vacillation in foreign policy (about 588 B.C). The "great eagle with great wings and long pinions" represents Nebuchadnezzar, second ruler of the neo-Babylonian Empire. In 598 B.C. he took the "topmost" of the young twigs (Jehoiachin), and carried him captive into "a land of trade" and "a city of merchants" (Mesopotamia). There this twig grew and prospered in rich soil until it became a spreading vine. There is every reason to accept the fact that Jehoiachin, though a prisoner, was given preferential treatment. Evidence for this conclusion is found in contemporary Babylonian records which list provisions for the king and in Jeremiah 52:31-34, where his release from prison is described.

"Another great eagle with great wings and much plumage" refers to Pharaoh Hophra (588-569 B.C.), but the "vine" in this case is Zedekiah, whose allegiance is transplanted to Egypt. The question then is: Will this transplanting grow and prosper? Its roots are said to be so shallow that neither "a strong arm" nor "many people" will be required to uproot it. In fact, when the east wind (a probable reference to Nebuchadnezzar) blows on it, it will quickly wither (vs. 10).

The second section of the chapter deals with the fact that Zedekiah (Mattaniah) had taken an oath of allegiance in the Lord's name. Reference to the captivity of 598 B.C. when king and princes were taken away introduces the fact that Nebuchadnezzar took "one of the seed royal and made a covenant with him, putting him under oath" (vs. 13). God's good name was involved since Zedekiah took a throne name which probably means "as surely as the Lord is righteous I will be loyal." By breaking his covenant of fealty to Nebuchadnezzar, Zedekiah impugned the name and character of the Lord (vs. 19). Because of this deception and distortion Zedekiah will die "in Babylon" (vs. 16). Moreover, the Egyptian armies which stimulated his defection from Chaldea will not help him in the distress of Jerusalem's siege. History tragically fulfilled these predictions that Zedekiah would die somewhere in Mesopotamia and that Egypt would give no help during the siege. After the capture of the king, his troops "shall be scattered to every wind" (vss. 20-21).

God will take "a sprig from the lofty top of the cedar" even as Nebuchadnezzar had done. The Lord will plant "a tender one" on the high mountain, and it will become a noble cedar under which the beasts of the field will dwell and in which the birds of the air will nest. The climax of the chapter and its most profound thought are summarized in the concluding verse: "And all the trees of the field shall know that I the LORD bring low the high tree, and make high the low tree, dry up the green tree, and make the dry tree flourish." Neither Nebuchadnezzar nor Pharaoh Hophra holds the key to history, however great their power. God decides among the nations of the earth.

Corporate Guilt and Individual Responsibility (18:1-32)

In a society where corporate life is the basic assumption of existence, a disruption of organized structure always has a devastating effect. Israel was an entity, God's people, worshiping as a people in God's house and with a national mission for God. With the disruption of life in its ordered corporate manifestation, there was need for an understanding of the individual's responsibility for inherited guilt.

The issue is clearly set in the words of a proverb which Ezekiel, who was always close to his people, heard repeatedly: "The fathers have eaten sour grapes, and the children's teeth are set on edge" (vs. 2). Obviously the plea is that Jerusalem in the early sixth century is a guiltless city, suffering unfairly for the sins of former generations. As the problem is set in a brief form, so the answer is given: "Behold, all souls are mine; the soul of the father as well as the soul of the son is mine: the soul that sins shall die" (vs. 4). God judges with discretion. Suffice it to say at this point, man has the power to transcend and rise above his heritage to the new heritage God will give; he need not be chained to a particular condition either by his heritage or by his surroundings. It is this that makes him truly man and not just another animal imprisoned by instinct and determined by heredity.

Verses 5-24 give more extensive evidence designed to demonstrate the principle that "the soul that sins shall die." Verses 5-9 list the characteristics of a righteous man who is promised life because of his fidelity. The criteria of righteousness are an interesting reflection of official morality, including: no idolatry, respect for a neighbor's wife, eschewing sexual relations during the menstrual period, no oppression, restoration of a pledged object to a debtor. Verses 10-13 present the reverse side of the same material, that is, those acts and attitudes which are unrighteous and because of which a man shall die regardless of how righteous his father was. Verses 14-18 come to grips with the problem brought on by the theory that a son begotten of an evil father need not suffer the same fate as his father. Summing up, the author concludes that the person who sins, be he father or son, is the one who stands condemned before the Lord.

Even for the wicked man, son or father, there is hope, because God's will is that man should live, not that he should die. Yet the man who has followed righteousness for a while dare not turn from righteousness and still expect God's blessing. In such a case past righteousness will have no bearing on God's judgment (vs. 24).

A complaint against the ways of the Lord is raised in the succinct outburst, "The way of the Lord is not just" (vs. 25). This kind of outcry against the Lord is understandable when we remember how great was the suffering and tragedy through which these people of God had passed. As always the prophet is a combined defender of God's ways and prosecutor of Israel's record. Turning the subject around, the prophet claims that the Lord stands always ready to punish iniquity and reward righteousness. This has been the consistent attitude of God and nothing has changed. The final question put to the listeners by the prophet is rhetorical: "Is it not your ways that are not just?" (vs. 29).

Like so many of the profound passages in Ezekiel, verses 30-32 combine doom and hope within the same breath. Everyone will be judged according to his ways; no one is condemned for what others have done. Because this is true God calls on the people through his prophet: "Repent and turn from all your transgressions, lest iniquity be your ruin" (vs. 30). Then they are advised to get themselves "a new heart and a new spirit." Previously, in 11:19-20, God promised to give the preserved remnant a new heart and a new spirit, while here he requires them to get these for themselves. The Israelite had such a sacramental understanding of life that it was impossible to separate God's act from man's response to it.

Verses 31b-32 remind us once more of Hosea. Ezekiel cries out, "Why will you die, O house of Israel? For I have no pleasure in the death of anyone, says the Lord GOD; so turn, and live." The Lord is not a capricious deity, enjoying the discomfort and tragedy of his creatures; on the contrary, he is heartbroken because they refuse the good life which he has proffered.

Parable of a Lioness and a Vine (19:1-14)

This chapter contains two allegories which deal with the same subject. Verses 1-9 refer to Judah as the lioness whose first whelp, Jehoahaz, learned to catch prey and devour men, only to be trapped and carried captive into Egypt. In point of historical fact, Jehoahaz, successor of Josiah (609 B.C.), remained on the throne for only three months, was deposed, possibly imprisoned, and replaced by Jehoiakim (609-598 B.C). Then the lioness Judah produced another whelp, Jehoiachin, who learned to catch prey and devour men, but because of his activities he, too, was no more heard in the mountains of Israel. We must not make this dirge fit every detail of history, since this was not its purpose, but in general it does follow the tragic trail of events.

Verses 10-14 have a literary resemblance to chapter 17. A sprawling vine is Judah which produces one strong stem, "a ruler's scepter" or a "scepter for a ruler," a clear reference to Zedekiah. The vine (Judah) is plucked up in fury and an east wind finishes the extermination by drying up the vine. What remains is a dried-up vine with neither foliage nor fruit, incapable of producing a stem strong enough to be a scepter. The country no longer has the strength or vitality to produce and to support her own ruler.

Prophecies Against the Land (20:1—24:27)

This final major section in the first half of the book repeats much that has already been said, while moving ever closer to the fulfillment of predicted doom. The whole scope of Judah's life is examined in review, and every element in society is brought into focus for condemnation by the Lord. The approach of Nebuchadnezzar is sensed as the indelible condition of Judah's black character is described.

Review of Judah's Sorry and Tragic History (20:1-44)

Various phases of the history of Judah and Jerusalem have been presented before in chapters 16, 17, and 19, but here the catalogue is plain and complete. Ezekiel, unlike some of his prophetic forebears, recognizes no time when the people were obedient to God. He believes rather that their whole history is the story of broken Covenant and disobedient life.

The date for this oracle is given in the same sequence as all other dates (see Introduction). The seventh year would be 591 B.C., when certain "elders of Israel," probably inhabitants of Telabib, came to sit with Ezekiel. The prophet would not talk to them on God's behalf because of their heritage of disobedience.

God made his Covenant with "the house of Jacob" while the people were captive in Egypt, revealing himself and promising to be the God of Jacob (Israel). This aggregation of clans became his people. Furthermore, God promised to bring Israel to a land of promise, "the most glorious of all lands" (vs. 6). The only requirement was that they free themselves from idols and other gods, since the Lord was their only God. Rebellion, however, was in their hearts even in Egypt, whose idols they never forsook.

In order to reveal his true nature among the nations, God did not let his people be destroyed in Egypt; rather he brought them out of bondage into the wilderness. Statutes, ordinances, and Sabbaths were given to them as memory devices, but to no avail. The Lord complains: "But the house of Israel rebelled against me in the wilderness" (vs. 13). In the wilderness the Lord again considered destroying a rebellious people, but for his name's sake he did not. His chief concern was to reveal himself through Israel as a God with interest in all nations.

Exhortation to change their way of life and turn from the ways of their fathers failed to awaken a true response in the children who entered the land of promise (vss. 18-21a). Threat of punishment and exile did not deter the headlong rush to serve idols. Since nothing else worked, God gave them over to false statutes and perverted ordinances, making them subject to the rules of Molech worship, in which it was necessary to offer the first-born by fire. Not even the horror of this false religion made them turn (vss. 21-26).

Coming into the land, they were enticed by the Canaanite fertility cults located on every high hill and under every leafy tree, where sacrifice was made. Canaanite gods had become the objects of worship; now the Lord would not bear their iniquity. The whole tragedy of Israel's history is caught in the saying, "Let us be like the nations, like the tribes of the countries, and worship wood and stone" (vs. 32). This is the sorry story of the conformity which the nation chose as a substitute for the opportunity God had given—the opportunity, as his people, to be especially useful to him.

God's case has been presented; now he will execute judgment upon the guilty even as he did in Egypt and in the wilderness (vss. 33-36). The people will pass under his rod even as sheep pass under the rod of their shepherd and will go in by number (vs. 37), but the rebels will be purged from among them (vs. 38). These rebellious ones shall not enter the land of Israel. The people of Israel are warned that they can serve their idols still, if that be their desire, but God will no more receive gifts from those whose true loyalty is to idols (vs. 39).

God does promise a return from exile and the restoration of the sacred offerings, with opportunity for all to serve him in obedience. Thus, God says, "I will manifest my holiness among you in the sight of the nations" (vs. 41). Once more the purpose of self-revelation to all nations is set forth. When the people have received the fulfillment of these promises, then they will be sorry for their wicked past (vs. 43). Then they will understand that the Lord is not finally motivated by their "evil ways" or "corrupt doings" but acts for the sake of his name. God is true to his purpose and character in all circumstances.

Judgment (20:45—21:32)

Not since chapters 4-7 and chapter 9 has the theme of judgment been presented with such force and thoroughness as it is in the following uninterrupted proclamation of doom. At least four oracles about the sword are intertwined in this passage: (1) The sword of the Lord unsheathed (20:45—21:7); (2) the song of the sword (21:8-17); (3) the sword of Nebuchadnezzar en route to Jerusalem (21:18-22); and (4) the sword of Chaldean conquest (21:28-32).

The prophet is instructed to turn his face southward toward the Negeb (the desert south of Hebron) and say to "the forest of the Negeb" (no trees grow in this region today) that a fire of destruction has been kindled which shall destroy the whole forest, green and dry trees alike. When this happens, men shall know that the Lord is the true God. At this juncture in his ministry Ezekiel heard his people's sardonic comments about his preaching. They were expressing mild contempt for his talk about forest fires with the question, "Is he not a maker of allegories?" (vs. 49).

The prophet, under divine instruction, then turns his face toward Jerusalem to preach against "the sanctuaries." God proclaims that he will draw forth his sword against "the land of Israel." Along with this news, Ezekiel receives the command to sigh with deep grief. When he is asked the reason for his sighing he will answer, "Because of the tidings. When it comes, every heart will melt and all hands will be feeble, every spirit will faint and all knees will be weak as water. Behold, it comes and it will be fulfilled" (vs. 7). This description of the reaction within Jerusalem to an attack from without closely parallels what has previously been said in 7:10-22. In the real crises of human history, man's power fails and only God can help.

Dramatic exultation over such tragedy is hardly what we could expect. The outburst in 21:8-17 must be understood in the light of the prophet's time and the whole conception of prophecy current then. Much prophecy from the time of King Saul on was given in an ecstatic state when all inhibition was cast aside and the prophet was under the compulsion of the divine Spirit. This ecstatic state was accompanied by rhythmic words and music, with some dancing. Ezekiel's dramatic exultation might have been accompanied by a sword dance of some kind. It is introduced with the exciting words found in verses 9 and 10. The sword is drawn by the Lord against his people and the princes of Israel. The words that follow are in the same mood and milieu as the display in 6:11-12, where rhythmic clapping of hands and movement of a sword back and forth accompany the words. The oracle ends as it began, with an unsheathed sword, busy at the slaughter to which God had directed it. The prophet's real exultation is in God's triumph over evil. To him the integrity of God, who is great beyond comprehension, and his true manifestation in history are absolutely primary.

Prediction now begins to blend into fulfillment (vss. 18-22). Nebuchadnezzar has started his approach from the north to attack the city of Jerusalem which has stubbornly resisted his rule. At a crossroads, the king of the Chaldeans must make a decision between attacking Rabbah of the Ammonites and turning his force against Jerusalem. Three means of divination were in use for such decisions at that time: shaking the arrows, consulting the teraphim, and looking at the liver (vs. 21). Leaving nothing to chance, the king is said to have followed all three methods. The exact technique and interpretation used in divination by the drawing of an arrow or the use of teraphim (household gods which were sometimes portable) we do not know. In Babylon the examination of the liver of a sacrificial animal was given priority. The lot fell out in favor of attacking Jerusalem. Although by the people of the city this is thought to be a false divination, capture is sure (vs. 23).

Verses 24-27 once more speak of the unforgiven sin of the people and direct scathing denunciation at Zedekiah, who is described as an "unhallowed wicked one" whose time of punishment has come. The turban and crown are removed and the kingdom shall be left in ruins until someone comes who has a right to rule.

Ammon had escaped the wrath of Nebuchadnezzar for the moment, but the wrath of the Lord would still be poured out on that nation. The same words used against Judah in the song of the sword are directed against the Ammonites. These people from across the Jordan had taken advantage of the disorganized and helpless state of Judah to pillage and plunder. As a result they now are condemned to be delivered into the "hands of brutal men, skilful to destroy." Ammonites will be like fuel for fire, and their blood will be shed in the midst of the land. Eventually marauders from the desert did reduce Ammon to impotence, all but blotting out her memory.

Catalogue of Jerusalem's Sins (22:1-31)

Jerusalem is called a "bloody city" because she "sheds blood in the midst of her" and "makes idols to defile herself" (vs. 3). Doubtless the reference is to the kind of social oppression against which Amos had spoken so strongly and to the idolatry which had been a real problem within Hebrew life for generations. Oppression and idolatry have brought near God's judgment, when people from far away will mock the infamous city which is so full of tumult.

"The princes of Israel" represent the leaders who remained in Jerusalem after the most prominent people of the land were carried captive in the surrender of 598 B.C. The sins of these leaders are catalogued. "Father and mother are treated with contempt"— a breach of commandment five (vs. 7). The sojourner, the fatherless, and the widow are mistreated—marking a significant departure from the tradition that one of the criteria for judgment of a society was the treatment of those who were defenseless. Holy things are despised and Sabbaths are broken. Slander, false worship, and various forms of immoral life darken the picture even more (vs. 9). Men "uncover their fathers' nakedness" (forbidden among the Hebrews) and have intercourse with a woman during her menstrual period (vs. 10). All sense of moral purity in the relationship between sexes has broken down. Men take bribes to bear false witness and so "to shed blood" and use their possessions to practice extortion. Princes set an incredibly unrighteous example before their people; small wonder that the fabric of society is rotten.

Verses 13-16 make three important points. First, the Lord will punish those whose prime purposes are dishonest gain and shed-

ding of blood. Economic and moral factors affect God's relationship to men. The Lord will not support a nation whose god is
gain and whose only moral law is license. The second implication
is even more compelling: "Can your courage endure, or can your
hands be strong, in the days that I shall deal with you?" The answer of experience is: No. Righteousness alone is the source of
national strength; apart from it, social order is debilitated by sin
and courage is diluted by immorality and duplicity. Finally, the
Almighty makes clear that he cannot and will not be neutral
under these circumstances, but will punish the culprits and destroy their "filthiness." His name will be profaned among the
nations, yet even in the face of this unfortunate result he will
send them into exile. Ordinarily Ezekiel explains much of God's
action on the supposition that the Almighty wishes at all costs to
avoid profanation of his name; that is, misunderstanding of his
Person and purpose.

Underlining the state of affairs in Jerusalem and Judah, the
prophet employs the figure of silver, bronze, tin, iron, and lead
in a crucible (vss. 17-22). Israel has become dross which must be
separated and melted out. Jerusalem is the crucible into which the
dross has been gathered for elimination. The nation and city shall
be melted by the wrath of God and the dross will be destroyed.
Whether there will be any remnant of pure metal remaining is not
stated.

If any glimmer of hope or flicker of confidence remains, it is
extinguished finally by an analysis of corruption in depth (22:23-
31). Without exception every responsible group in the social order
has become irresponsible. Princes are not motivated by service,
but are like "a roaring lion" with a voracious appetite, caring
more for their possessions than for their subjects (vs. 25). Priests,
whose function it was to study the Law and protect the holy vessels of God in the Temple, have done violence to the Law, disre-
garding the separation of the clean from the unclean, making no
distinction between the common and the holy (vs. 26). Verse 27
repeats the earlier indictment of the princes. Prophets have seen
false visions and performed lying divinations, and when the wall
of Israel's life was crumbling, they have daubed it with whitewash, pretending that weakness was strength (vs. 28; see 13:8-
16). "The people of the land" have practiced extortion, committed robbery, and oppressed the poor, the needy, and the sojourner. When the roll call is finished, there is no group which

is worthy; hence, there is no basis for the continuance of Judah's existence, whose reason for being has been destroyed. The full force of the chapter's meaning is summarized in verse 30, "And I sought for a man among them who should build up the wall and stand in the breach before me for the land, that I should not destroy it; but I found none." Doubtless this statement, like Elijah's "I, even I only, am left" (I Kings 19:10), is an exaggeration, because there were good men in Jerusalem, including Jeremiah, but overstatement was the prophetic method of dramatizing a dangerous situation. Inevitably doom is the next step after a nation in rebellion loses its reason for being and ignores its commission from God.

Story of Two Sisters (23:1-49)

There can be little doubt that this remarkable and somewhat shocking chapter is a piece with chapter 16, which presented in a vivid allegory the history of an unfaithful land. The symbol of marriage as descriptive of God's relationship to his people was not new, but was used sparingly in Israel because of its similarity to a Baal fertility concept. From the era of Hosea onward, however, the ideas of God as father and as husband were variously used by the leaders of Hebrew thought. In this chapter he is husband; the paramours of Judah are her foreign alliances which had spiritual as well as political implications. Details of the punishment to be inflicted upon these wayward women is the theme of the latter part of the chapter. Even modern readers are generally shocked by the unabashed erotic descriptions which are used in the chapter and the cruel, unrelenting punishment of women caught in the circumstance of infidelity. It should be remembered that Ezekiel is using the normal thought forms and habit patterns of his day to carry weighty teachings about God's ways with men.

Two women, daughters of one mother, have "played the harlot" from their youth, a reference to infidelity during Egyptian enslavement. No doubt is left as to the meaning of Ezekiel's words after the details of intimacy are spelled out in verse 3. Oholah, the older sister, is identified with Samaria. The name means "she who has a tent." Oholibah, the younger sister, is identified with Jerusalem and her name means "tent in her." The symbolic names are almost surely designed to call attention to the tents set up for sacred prostitution at Baal shrines, and as such refer again to the basic infidelity of Judah's life (vss. 1-4).

The record of the older sister is first reviewed in some detail. While Oholah was wife to the Lord she played the harlot with the Assyrians, being enamored with that nation's purple-clad troops, its leaders, and its desirable young men. Assyrians struck terror in Jewish hearts but at the same time were secretly admired. This kind of infidelity was not new with the people, for such had been the pattern since their national youth in Egypt (vss. 5-10).

The older sister is brought into the account for comparative purposes. Samaria had been in ruins since 721 B.C., when Sargon had done his work well. Already her people were an ethnic mixture who were held in contempt by the Jews. Her record of infidelity was thought to be the worst possible. Yet Ezekiel says that Oholibah (Jerusalem) is far more degraded than Oholah (Samaria) ever was. After doting on Assyria—being enamored of the Assyrian way of life and worship—Judah turned her devotion and affection to the Chaldeans without any compunction. She openly flaunted "her nakedness" and "harlotry," which caused God finally to cast her off (vss. 11-18). The underlying historical situation or situations to which the prophet has reference cannot be finally or accurately identified, but it is certain that the object of derision is Judah's willingness to bend to the strongest wind of political power, which at the moment was Chaldea.

Ezekiel strikes the note of doom when he repeats his earlier allegation that the pattern of Judah's life had not really changed since she was in Egypt. Uncontrollable desire had always marked her life since her youth among the Egyptians. The love of Oholibah was not for her husband, but for a multiplicity of paramours, whom she received without discretion or shame. Thus syncretism in politics led to the tragedy of moral deterioration and spiritual decay.

Oholibah, who has been loved by many, now has all her lovers turn on her in disgust, seeking vengeance on her who had given herself to every passer-by. Babylonians and Assyrians join in meting out the punishment prescribed in Israel for the infidelity of a wife. She is stripped naked (vs. 26) and is mutilated before witnesses (vs. 25), having her nose and ears cut off. All her jewels and possessions are taken and she is left attractive to nobody, naked and bare, without help or friendship. The nature of Judah's sin is revealed in verse 30 where she is said to have "polluted" herself "with their idols." The prophet does not present either a logical or a chronological sequence for the punishment of this woman. After he has described her humiliation he speaks of the cup of God's wrath which is given to her to drink. The cup is identical with the cup from which Oholah has already drunk. The final result of it is madness (vss. 33b-34). This is the consequence of Judah's playing a double role on the stage of history—pretending to be God's peculiar people while lusting after and imitating the ways of pagan neighbors, depending upon their power, not God's, for support.

The oracle in verses 37-49 must be understood as a different piece from the Oholah-Oholibah story. It deals concurrently with both sisters as if punishment were impending for both. They are considered together, probably as a result of Ezekiel's unwillingness to accept the division between Israel and Judah as either valid or final. Both are accused of identical crimes: defiling God's sanctuary, breaking the Sabbath, and sacrificing children to foreign gods. While they were actually involved in false religion, Samaria and Jerusalem had maintained the appearance of fidelity to God (vss. 37-38). Returning to the figure of harlotry the prophet depicts in most lurid terms the ends to which lust has dragged a people. Indictment is followed immediately by execution. Any man having relations with either sister is guilty of adultery. So righteous men shall judge both for their crimes. Stoning and disfiguring, or even dismemberment, are prescribed in order that "sinful idolatry" may be at an end. Ezekiel understands that once individual man or society turns from God's love, the result is destruction.

Last Days of Jerusalem (24:1-27)

In verses 1-14 the terrible day of attack has begun, and all the horrors of siege are brought into bold relief by a prophetic image. "The ninth year, in the tenth month" would be 588 B.C., when Nebuchadnezzar attacked the city. The prophetic description takes the form of an allegory in which Jerusalem is a pot and its people are flesh seething over a hot fire (vss. 3-5). Suddenly the rusty pot is emptied but is left on the fire that fire may purge it of corruption. At this point there is confusion between the two allegories, one a pot with meat seething and the other an empty pot being purified by fire. After verse 10 the pot is empty because the inhabitants have been thoroughly destroyed, and the pot is left to burn itself clean (vs. 11). But the rust and corrosion have become too much a part of the pot, and the fire cannot separate it from its corrosion. The rust is identified as "lewdness," that is, "idolatry." Because the rust is so ingrained—that is to say, because idolatry has become so much a part of Jerusalem's way of life—God will not cancel the fury of destruction (vss. 13-14). The tragedy of national sins, which began as occasional lapses but became part and parcel of a way of life, is the essence of a tragedy which not even God will redeem.

As with Hosea and Isaiah before him, Ezekiel's domestic life became a means for emphasizing his spiritual mission (vss. 15-24). Ezekiel's wife died in the evening after he had been warned of this blow. He was instructed to forego the usual rites of mourning and to continue his daily life as if nothing had happened (vss. 15-18).

When people inquired of the prophet about his strangely eccentric behavior, he explained that his lack of grief was no more unusual than what would take place at the impending tragedy in Jerusalem, whose dimensions are to be far greater than his own domestic life. Facing a destructive and chaotic immediate future, nobody showed any sign of grief or repentance (vs. 23). Ezekiel thus became a sign to Judah by foregoing any demonstration of grief when his wife died. He saw that the tragedy about to overwhelm his whole nation was far deeper than his personal loss.

On the day when the corporate tragedy shall come upon the city and the Temple ("the delight of their eyes"), a fugitive will come to Ezekiel from the city (vss. 25-27). Then the prophet will be able to speak openly and not be so taciturn as he had been in this prelude to disaster. When his mouth was opened, Ezekiel was apparently free to speak to the doomed people of hope and resurrection. Chronologically 33:21-22 should immediately follow 24:27, as even a cursory reading will clearly show. In any case, at the end of chapter 24 the blow has fallen and Ezekiel's sorrowful task as a prophet of doom is complete. Following a section directed against the foreign nations (chs. 25-32), the prophet of doom becomes dominantly a harbinger of hope and restoration.

PROPHECIES AGAINST FOREIGN NATIONS
Ezekiel 25:1—32:32

The second major division of the prophecy is the natural outgrowth of the expansive vision which opened the ministry of

Ezekiel and of the great theme which underlies his writing. God —who can no longer be identified with Palestine alone, who can be met in the Mesopotamian mudflats in a summer storm, who can withdraw from Jerusalem to go where he will—is a God who by his very nature relates himself to all nations.

These oracles serve to establish two concepts very clearly: first, all mankind is morally and spiritually responsible to Almighty God; second, no nation will escape the responsibility to obey the common laws of humanity. Neither imperial greatness (Tyre and Egypt) nor insignificant powerlessness (Ammon, Edom, and the like) could mean that judgment would be withheld.

Immediate Neighbors of Judah (25:1-17)

Ammon (25:1-7)

The contempt in which Ammon was held by the Hebrews is best reflected in the account of this nation's origin, which explains that Ammon is the issue of the drunken, incestuous activity of Lot (Gen. 19:30-38). Subsequent history unfolded a series of incidents which deepened the enmity between the two neighboring states (for example, Judges 11:4-33; I Sam. 11:1-4; 14:47; II Sam. 8:11-12; 10:1-14). In Judah's present extremity Ammon showed great delight at the tragedy which had befallen God's people, not because the tragedy vindicated God, but because it satisfied a sadistic bestiality in the Ammonites.

The warning to the culprit Ammon is that marauders from the East will dwell in her land, which will become a "pasture for camels"; her cities will be a "fold for flocks" (vs. 5). Because Ammon has enjoyed the grief of others, she shall herself be brought to grief. In such action God will reveal that behind all events stands the Author and Finisher of history, who becomes Judge of all men and nations.

Moab (25:8-11)

Moab showed herself to be insensitive to the peculiarity of Judah's mission, saying, "Judah is like all the other nations." When this people, who had a long history of violence against Judah, saw the land destroyed they were delighted that the Hebrews did not have, as they had claimed, the special blessing and protection of God. Since Moab had rejoiced she, too, would be invaded and her cities destroyed.

Edom (25:12-14)

Judah's third neighbor, Edom, whose kinship with the Hebrews is traced back to the Esau-Jacob cycle of stories in Genesis, was guilty of taking vengeance upon the house of Judah, apparently during a period when Judah was helpless against attack. This vengeance was not of God, hence it offended him. The whole country of Edom is consigned to desolation from one end to the other (from Teman to Dedan), and God's vengeance will be meted out by the hand of his people Israel. This became a reality during the Maccabean ascendancy in the second century B.C. Those who arrogate to themselves the vengeance of God will quickly learn what God's vengeance really is (vs. 14).

Philistia (25:15-17)

Since the period of the Judges, "never-ending enmity" had existed between the Hebrews and the Philistines and related sea peoples ("Cherethites"). Because the remnants of Philistia had taken advantage of Judah in the past, destruction now casts a heavy shadow on their future. The brief oracle, however, is not as vibrant with anger as the previous three oracles.

Tyre (26:1—28:23)

Tyre was a center of extensive commerce from the days of David and Solomon, when it became the seat of Phoenician power. The city, built on an island connected to the mainland only by a causeway, was almost impregnable from land attack. Widespread Assyrian conquest, which swept everything before it, did not overwhelm this city. Even the Egyptian dominance by Pharaoh Hophra, who forced its surrender (588 B.C.) without capture, was short-lived. After his successful destruction of Jerusalem, Nebuchadnezzar turned his full might against the island stronghold. After thirteen years of siege (585-573 B.C.) the city still stood proud in solitary strength and was given favorable terms by the frustrated Chaldean hosts. Since Ezekiel had clearly predicted the capture of the city and its utter destruction, the prophet does something that prophets seldom do: he admits that the prophecy was not fulfilled (29:18-20). It remained for Alexander the Great to conquer this city by combined attack from land and sea.

Destruction Foretold (26:1-14)

It is obvious that this oracle should be dated after the fall of Jerusalem, which means that "the eleventh year" must be read "the twelfth year," as in 33:21. On this occasion Tyre is pictured gloating over her opportunity for gain at the expense of fallen Jerusalem. This predatory nature, already condemned in Ammon and Moab, is denounced also in Tyre. Destruction at the hands of many nations is forecast for the proud city, so that it will become a denuded island in the sea where nets are spread to dry. Utter destruction of the island is forecast, as well as annihilation of Tyrians in the mainland villages ("daughters").

Nebuchadnezzar is named as the historical personage who will execute the judgment of God on the proud island fortress. First, the Chaldeans will destroy the Tyrian suburbs on the mainland; then, as Esarhaddon, the Assyrian, had done in the previous century, mounds will be raised against the city. The noise and chaotic movement of horses, chariots, and battering rams are felt in the words of verses 9-10, while death, destruction, and pillage come to mind in verses 11-12. Every sign of mirth and happiness will cease. No songs will be sung, nor will the lyre be heard. The rock island city will become a bare rock where fishermen will leave their nets to dry, and no rebuilding will take place. The gaunt remains of ancient Tyre hauntingly remind one of this prediction! The word of God's judgment has gone forth and has surely come to pass.

Effect on Other Nations (26:15-18)

Tyre had become a sign of impregnability among the nations. When all else changed, Tyre remained majestically aloof in her island retreat. News of her fall will have devastating effect upon peoples everywhere, even as the fall of France in 1940 had a crushing and almost disastrous effect upon the modern Western world. Princes of the sea—that is, leaders of the sea peoples—shall be afraid and shall go into mourning at the terrible news that Tyre is destroyed.

No Memory of Tyre (26:19-21)

One must understand the dimensions of ancient man's thought to comprehend what the prophet is saying to the city of Tyre in this passage. From earliest times life had risen out of the "deep," over which God brooded in creation. Return to Sheol or the Pit meant a reversion to a shadowy state of lifelessness. Ezekiel consigns Tyre to the Pit and banishes her from "the land of the living." She will go down with the "people of old" amid the ruins of lost societies and civilizations.

Lament Over Tyre (27:1-36)

The city is likened unto a ship whose builders have made her perfect in beauty with materials drawn from many places: fir trees from Senir, a cedar from Lebanon, oaks from Bashan, pines from Cyprus, linen from Egypt, and dye from the seacoasts (vss. 5-7). Her builders, rowers, and pilots have also been drawn from other nations. Much of the skill and raw material of the ancient world had been combined to enrich Tyre (vss. 8-9). After the interruption of verses 10-25a the poem resumes.

The ship, heavily laden with much cargo in the midst of a stormy sea, is wrecked. All the skilled men of Tyrian trade go down with the ship. Outcries from the stricken ship cause terror and mourning on the shore. Contrast the greatness that was Tyre (vs. 33) with the desolation that Tyre has become (vs. 34). The psychological shock was almost too much for the ancient world to bear (vss. 35-36).

Verses 10-25a are an editorial insertion placed in the midst of the poem to detail how extensive and multifarious Tyrian trade was. Place names and materials traded are presented in dazzling array.

Overthrow of a Proud King (28:1-10)

The prince of Tyre had committed the horrible blasphemy, common to every tyrant, of equating himself with deity in wisdom and power. He sat "in the seat of the gods," thinking of himself as a deity on earth. "You are indeed wiser than Daniel" is pure sarcasm. The Daniel referred to in this passage is a certain "Dan'el" in antiquity who was famous for his sagacity. The king had been successful in his trade, hence he was convinced that he was divine. God's judgment, however, would come upon such undue pride in human wisdom. Again, Tyre is not only delivered to the destroyers on history's stage, but she is also consigned to the Pit, to Sheol, the place of darkness and death, the primeval chaos (vss. 6-10).

Lamentations Over the King (28:11-19)

The second phase of this chapter is cast in the framework of creation and the idyllic beauty of Eden, "the garden of God," where Tyre is said to have been placed and given every advantage. The ostentatious descriptions of precious stones must be recognized as symbolic of the rich and priceless heritage which belonged to the king. A cherubic (angelic) guard protected him, and for a time Tyre was "blameless." This is obviously no description of a simple flesh-and-blood man but is rather an idealization in terms reminiscent of Adam in the Garden of Eden (vss. 12-15).

The city's downfall from an idyllic state and a blameless life is laid to the "abundance of trade," apparently a predilection for possessions. Because this happened God cast Tyre off as "a profane thing," and the guardian cherub, even as he had driven Adam out of the garden, drove the king out of his Eden of privilege. Again Tyre is consigned to destruction and her pride in her former glory is reduced to dust and ashes (vss. 18-19).

Against Sidon (28:20-23)

The reason for the inclusion of this brief passage against Sidon is not far to seek, for Sidon was ordinarily associated with Tyre as the dominant center of Phoenician power. It is apparently assumed that the reasons for its judgment are identical with those described in the indictment of Tyre. The main purpose of this separate oracle is to fix the judgment of God upon Sidon along with Tyre.

Editorial Interlude: Restoration of Israel (28:24-26)

Verse 24 is a postscript to the oracles against Tyre and Sidon whose removal has cleared the way for Israelite restoration, which state of blessedness the prophet proceeds to describe. When Israel is restored she will be brought back from captivity into territory given to Jacob (Israel). The land had long since been identified as the permanent possession of Israel's descendants. They shall dwell securely in the land, following the traditional occupations of building and husbandry (vs. 26). This tranquillity is made possible because God has executed his judgments upon their neighbors, who had been "a brier to prick . . . a thorn to hurt" (vs. 24). Like every other mighty act of God's judgment or of his redemption, this event shall reveal to all men who he really is.

Egypt (29:1—32:32)

Prophecy Against Egypt (29:1-16)

Tyre, as the chief center of seagoing commerce, could be symbolized by a ship, and her destruction could be spelled out in terms of a sinking ship. In similar fashion Egypt's life was so closely associated with the Nile River that "the great dragon" (crocodile) came to represent Egypt. In a poetic oracle Ezekiel proclaims that this crocodile, Egypt, will be captured, dragged ashore, and left on the open land to provide birds and beasts their food (vss. 3-5). Explanation for this harsh execution is given in a prose passage immediately following the poetic oracle. The unreliability of Egypt as an ally of Israel and her vacillation in foreign relations are the chief items in the indictment. When the house of Israel reached toward Egypt as a staff for strength, it proved to be a brittle reed which broke when weight was put on it, causing considerable injury to Israel. Certainly Judah's and Israel's dependence upon Egypt in former times had proved disastrous (see Isa. 36:6; II Kings 18:21). Even as late as the siege of Jerusalem, groundless hope for rescue from siege had been raised by an Egyptian diversionary thrust from the south (see Jer. 37).

Egypt in great pride claimed with unequaled egotism, "My Nile is my own; I made it." The ultimate human madness arises when men begin to take credit for their own origin. Because of pride which leaves God out of creation itself the Lord promises to sweep the land from Migdol on the Delta in the north to the first cataract of the Nile at Syene in the south, that is, from one end of the country to the other. For forty years (one generation) the land of the Nile shall lie desolate. During those forty years a general dispersion of the Egyptians among the nations will occur.

God promises restoration to the Egyptians, but it is a restoration to humiliation wherein they will never again be permitted to gain an exalted position or rule in harshness over their neighbors. In the world where Israel is to be dominant, Egypt will exist, but she will no longer menace others.

Egypt, the Prize for Nebuchadnezzar (29:17-21)

Nebuchadnezzar besieged Tyre for about thirteen years (585-572 B.C.) without capturing the island fortress. Because the Chaldean leader had "made his army labor hard against Tyre" in this manner without "pay for the labor he had performed," God promised to give Egypt to the Chaldeans. Note that this oracle is dated in the twenty-seventh year (about 571 B.C.), after the siege of Tyre had been lifted and peace terms had been drawn. This prose passage was doubtless added to the collection in the thirtieth year as an explanation of the nonfulfillment of an earlier prediction that Tyre would be destroyed. Egypt will be Nebuchadnezzar's recompense. Jeremiah had earlier predicted the destruction of Egypt at the hands of the Chaldean army (Jer. 43:8-13; 46:1-26). Nebuchadnezzar did invade Egypt in 568-567 B.C., but the shadow of his power on the Nile was short-lived.

Verse 21 appears to be a later editorial comment. It has some relationship to the prophet's strange silence which will end when a horn (Messiah) arises after Egypt has fallen.

Destruction of Egypt Rehearsed (30:1-19)

The Day of the Lord draws near and casts its pall of doom over the nations, including Egypt. Egypt, Ethiopia (the ruling dynasty of Egypt at this time was Ethiopian), and surrounding areas will be brought low by the destructive fury of God. This will happen in Egypt because of her pride; she will become a desolation in the midst of other desolate countries (vss. 6-8). This judgment will be carried out by the hand of Nebuchadnezzar, who is God's instrument of destruction. The land of the Nile shall be destroyed, its people slain, and even the river itself, the source of life, shall be dried up (vss. 10-12). The reason for utter destruction follows. Idolatry is the key to disaster, and of course idolatry is pride in action. Every center of culture and political power (Memphis, Zoan, Thebes, Pelusium, and others) is listed to show how inclusive the judgment shall be. None shall be spared, so that the "proud might" of Egypt shall be brought to an inglorious end (vss. 18-19).

The Broken Arms of Egypt (30:20-26)

The "arm" of Egypt has been broken by the Lord and has not been bound up, lest in healing it might regain its former awesome strength. One arm has been broken, now the other shall be similarly fractured, leaving Egypt helpless when the king of Babylon attacks (vss. 22-24). Pharaoh and Egypt shall groan before Nebuchadnezzar as a dying man groans in weakness. But even while the Lord breaks the arms of Egypt, he promises strength to the arms of the king of Babylon, which are stretched out to destroy Egypt. The residue of the Egyptians, after destruction, will be scattered. It is God who breaks or strengthens in history. Behind the power which men think rules in history, stands God, the true ruler.

Elimination of the Tall Cedar (31:1-18)

With yet another figure, the prophet describes the judgment of God upon Egypt. In this instance the Nile empire is likened unto a tall cedar tree in whose branches birds live and under whose shade the beasts rest (vs. 6). Greater than the cedars of Lebanon (vs. 3), superior to the cedars in the garden of God (vs. 8), and watered by the rivers, the tree is envied by all other trees of creation. This oracle is similar to the concept found in chapter 28, which relates the king of Tyre to creation and to Eden.

The tree, because of its pride in height and beauty, will be utterly destroyed (vss. 10-13) and its remains will be sent to the region of the dead (the Pit). Such contemptible arrogance will not again occur. When Egypt descends into the Pit, there will be mourning and great fear among the nations. "The trees of Eden" represent the peoples of God's creation, because these who dwell under the shadow of Egyptian protection will be destroyed also (vs. 17). The tree will be destroyed and thrust into Sheol forever. To make sure that nobody misunderstands what Ezekiel is talking about, a footnote has been added: "This is Pharaoh and all his multitude, says the Lord GOD" (vs. 18b).

Dirge Over Pharaoh and Egypt (32:1-16)

Chapter 32 returns to the motif of the river monster which appeared in 29:3-5, accusing Pharaoh of being a dragon in the waters which he troubles and fouls with his feet. Much as in chapter 29, the dragon is doomed to be caught in God's net and cast upon the open field where the beasts and birds gorge themselves on his dead flesh (vss. 3-4). The flesh of the monster will be strewn over the mountains and his blood will flow in the valleys (vss. 5-6). Verses 7-8 describe the cataclysmic effect of Egypt's destruction on nature and are representative of the emerging prophetic language used to describe nature's reaction to the Lord's intervention in history.

A prose section (vss. 9-12a) describes the effect upon nations who hear that the monster has fallen. Once again the description, though stylized, is an accurate representation of the troubled reaction which arose among the nations at Egypt's fall.

The poem or lament resumes with verse 12b, where the extent of the destruction is related. Waters which have been troubled and fouled by Egypt will run clear again once this troublemaker is banished from the face of the earth.

Verse 16 explains that the lamentation (vss. 2-8, 12b-15) will be sung by the daughters of the nations over prostrate Egypt. Not only will Egypt fall; she also will become the subject of a sorrowful lament.

Descent Into Sheol (32:17-32)

Like Tyre before her, Egypt will go into Sheol, the land of darkness and shadowy existence. Her beauty will be brought to the depths reserved for the uncircumcised, and her multitudes will be sent into Sheol (vss. 17-21). Among the inhabitants who have preceded Egypt to Sheol is Assyria, whose graves are in the uttermost parts of the Pit because they "spread terror in the land of the living" (vss. 22-23). Elam is there also (vss. 24-25), as are Meshech and Tubal (Asia Minor cities); and Edom has been brought into the same Pit. Princes from the north (that is, Armenia) and the Sidonians are among the ghostly company. Pharaoh joins this infamous aggregation whose crime is against humanity (they "spread terror in the land of the living"). Because of this they will be consigned to Sheol and will no longer be privileged with life, which they had made so miserable for others. The inexorable law and purpose of God are at work in all places, with no exception made for the allegedly great.

PROPHECIES OF HOPE

Ezekiel 33:1—39:29

These seven chapters—in no sense a cohesive unit—are held together by an emerging and increasingly dominant note of hope. In order to remove any possible fear of the future, the author pictures the world as it will be subsequent to restoration, and in vision he sees a great cosmic struggle in which the ends of the earth will rise up against God and his people but will be defeated.

Editorial Review of Former Oracles (33:1-33)

This chapter is a literary binder which is fashioned for the express purpose of uniting chapters 1-24 with chapters 34-39, giving basis for future hope and restoration. The watchman motif is repeated (compare 33:1-9 and 3:16-21), and the problem of individual responsibility is again presented (compare 33:10-20 and ch. 18). Verses 23-29 appear to be a shorter form of 20:14-21. In the midst of these repetitions there is set a date which chronologically belongs after 24:27 (33:21-22). Added to this is a fascinating glimpse into the popularity of the prophet, the only new material included in the chapter (vss. 30-33).

Call to Be a Watchman (33:1-9)

The substance of this oracle is identical with the charge or commission given to the prophet at the outset in 3:16-21. A prophet must warn his people of impending judgment, then if disaster does come the responsibility is theirs, not his. Otherwise, failing to warn the people of impending disaster, the prophet bears responsibility and guilt. To such a task Ezekiel was called.

Corporate Guilt and Individual Responsibility (33:10-20)

This section is essentially a repetition of chapter 18, which has been discussed at some length. Sometimes the verses are identical with the expression found in the longer presentation, while in other parts they are a condensation. The problem of individual responsibility arose naturally at a time when corporate life was disintegrating. Prophetic preaching had explained this dissolution as a result of corporate guilt. Ezekiel emphasizes individual responsibility within the framework of corporate life, and stresses the fact that the Lord does not desire the death of any corporate or individual life.

A Chronological Note (33:21-22)

By a simple shift of letters in the Hebrew text "the twelfth year" becomes "the eleventh year," which is almost certainly correct (vs. 21). That was the year Jerusalem fell and word of the disaster came to the prophet through an escapee from the doomed city. In chronological order these verses would immediately follow 24:27. Ezekiel was generally a silent prophet, except on those occasions when his mouth was opened by the Lord. With the fall of Jerusalem, the prophet recovered from the dumbness which had come upon him in "the plain" when he received the commission from God (3:22-27). The prophet henceforth is a harbinger of hope, not a disciple of despair.

Reason for Jerusalem's Destruction (33:23-29)

The old problem of who constitutes the People of God—that is, who are to be the inheritors of the land—lies back of this passage. People living in waste places within Palestine claimed that the land by right belonged to them because it had been given to Abraham, their father. Ezekiel, like Jeremiah before him (Jer. 24), pinned his hope for the future on the exiles, not upon the people of the land. To explain why these folk were disinherited, Ezekiel reads the particulars of their indictment, and follows that with a description of judgment by the sword, wild beasts, and pestilence. The end of the process will leave the land in a state of utter waste. Then they shall know that the Lord is truly God of heaven and earth.

Hearers Who Do Listen (33:30-33)

The meaning here is obvious. Hearing with their ears, the people do not understand with their hearts. Ezekiel personally becomes a center of great popular interest among the exiles. But those who come and sit attentively listening, "with their lips . . . show much love, but their heart is set on their gain" (vs. 31b). They are pleased with the melodious voice of the prophet, who is like a singer of songs or a player of a musical instrument. To hear him conjures up visions of a better day, but what he is saying does not affect their understanding or influence their life. When the prophetic word is fulfilled, they will know that the voice among them was that of God's prophet. Then the ministry of Ezekiel will be vindicated.

Future Promise (34:1—37:28)

A series of unrelated oracles cluster together, united by a single magnetic hope. Chapter 35 is a denunciation of Edom with a prediction of doom, but this is only a prelude to a complete restoration of Judah and Israel.

Shepherds and a Shepherd (34:1-31)

The shepherd figure is dominant in the life and thought of the Hebrew people, who were essentially a shepherd people. David was a shepherd king, drawn from tending the flock to be king. Frequently the king is described as the shepherd of his people. The Lord is pictured in this manner on certain occasions (for example, Ps. 80:1). In time the Messiah is described as the Shepherd of God's true people, as is the case in Ezekiel.

The chapter opens with a condemnation of the shepherds of Israel, the kings of the land who have been set over the flock by the direction of God. Indictment of these monarchs is severe. They feed themselves, not the sheep; they eat fat and clothe themselves with wool; they have neither helped the weak nor healed the sick; the strayed, the scattered, and the lost have not been brought back; and above all, the shepherds have not even sought their sheep (vss. 2-6). The same kind of denunciation is leveled against the kings by Jeremiah (Jer. 23:1-4) and also earlier by the prophet Micah (Micah 3:1-3, 11). What disturbed the prophet and initiated the judgment of God was the fact that the kings of Israel and Judah, dedicated to the service of their people by the Lord's anointing, had become little more than oriental potentates, living in luxury, caring nothing for their subjects.

In keeping with well-worked-out patterns, indictment is followed by judgment. Because of their selfish aggrandizement at the expense of a scattered and lost people, God is against the shepherds who have had no care for his people. They will no longer be shepherds, feeding themselves on the flock of God, because the Almighty will rescue his sheep out of their ravenous mouths (vss. 7-10).

God proclaims that he will be shepherd of his sheep (vss. 11-24; compare Psalm 23 and John 10:1-18). God will perform the office of shepherd for his people who have been forsaken by their kings, and he will rule over them in mercy. They will be gathered in from the far places and fed by his hand. In summary, the prophet says for God these unforgettable words: "I myself will be the shepherd of my sheep, and I will make them lie down" (vss. 15-16). This promise of security to an uprooted people is more dramatic than we, from our vantage point, could know. The full ministry of God is described in these terms: "I will seek the lost, and I will bring back the strayed, and I will bind up the crippled, and I will strengthen the weak, and the fat and the strong I will watch over; I will feed them in justice" (vs. 16).

Reference to the fat and the strong reminds the writer of the differences that exist and persist within God's own flock. God promises to judge between sheep and sheep, between rams and he-goats. Some sheep eat all they want, drink all they want, and then trample the grass and foul the water, so that none can eat or drink afterward (vss. 18-19). This apparently is a reference to the rulers who wasted the substance of the land while others went in want.

God not only judges a flock; he determines the quality of life in the individual sheep. Corporate righteousness does not wipe out the individual guilt of those who are irresponsible and self-centered in that corporate life. Those who are strong and who push with their shoulder will be judged. The flock as a whole, however, will be redeemed from external dangers and internal tensions. Over the renewed and restored flock there will be one Shepherd, "my servant David." This reference is doubtless Messianic in direction and implication. God, who earlier said he would himself be Shepherd, now appoints "David" to the task. There is no contradiction, however, since God remains their God and ultimately their Shepherd, whose shepherding care is to be exercised through the New David, his anointed, the Messiah (vs. 24).

It is not enough that the bad kings be banished and the Messiah established; the basic Covenant relationship must also be renewed on a permanent basis. God promises "a covenant of peace," which means both the absence of danger from marauding beasts and also security in a land of blessing and abundance (vss. 26-27). Blessings will come like showers; the yoke of slavery will be removed; they will no more experience hunger or be a reproach among all the nations.

In this blessed state of renewal and restoration the people so benefited will know that the Lord is truly God upon whom they can depend. The whole substance of the chapter is summed up in the closing verse: "And you are my sheep, the sheep of my pasture, and I am your God . . ." The Covenant relationship between God and his people will be firmly reconstituted and the happy issue will be a transformed life and society.

Edom Destroyed (35:1-15)

Edom, who was guilty of a "perpetual enmity" against Judah, is marked for destruction because she has taken advantage of Judah in the time of that nation's calamity. The prophet had already discussed Edom (25:12-14) but apparently felt that her crimes were so scarlet as to require more detailed treatment. Traditionally descended from Esau, the twin brother of Jacob from whose lineage the Israelites came, Edom had long been despised by them. Other prophets bore the same grudge against "Mount Seir," an alternate name for Edom (Isa. 34:1-17; Jer. 49:7-22; Mal. 1:2-5; Obad. 1-14).

The crime of which Edom is accused is that of "perpetual enmity." That nation, out of the desire to possess for herself the territory of both Israel and Judah, took advantage of fallen Judah (vs. 10). On the occasion of Jerusalem's fall Edom had said, "They are laid desolate, they are given us to devour" (vs. 12b). In this oracle there is a mixture of indictment and announcement of judgment which leads one to think that the chapter is a collection of short sayings about Edom with editorial binders. Edom will be repaid in precisely the same coin that she gave. Our judgments against others are frequently made into boomerangs by the hand of the Lord. A later Voice made this fact of life very clear when he said that according as we measure, we ourselves shall be measured (Matt. 7:1-2).

Destruction and Restoration (36:1-38)

First the prophet deals with the coming end to national shame (vss. 1-15). Because of the humiliation and tragedy of defeat, Israel had become "the talk and evil gossip of the people" (vs. 3). Enemies had gloated over possessing the ancient heights of Jerusalem, and every reason that Israel had to think of herself as distinctive had been blotted out. Speaking to the mountains, the ravines, and the desolate waste of deserted cities, God now promises that his destructive wrath shall be turned against other nations who like Edom rejoiced in the tragedy. Because the surrounding nations had rejoiced in destruction, which gave them opportunity for pillaging and for booty, these nations shall now suffer the same reproach (vss. 5-7).

These same mountains, hills, and ravines which were left desolate and waste by the hordes of Nebuchadnezzar would soon be reoccupied by a restored and renewed Israel. Cities are to be inhabited and waste places rebuilt. Israel will walk in her own promised land again, and her children will not be taken from her. The past habits which had brought disaster will be expunged from society and the people will neither be a reproach nor bear the disgrace of destruction. The cause will be removed and the effect will be taken away (vss. 8-15).

At this juncture Ezekiel begins to deal with the most popular and pressing theological problem which arose out of the destruction of Jerusalem and the experience of the Exile. It was plain to see that Judah's sin, her abrogation of the Covenant, was the basis for judgment, and rightly so. That she got her just deserts was grudgingly admitted under the guidance of prophetic instruction. But the neighboring nations knew only that these folk who were supposed to be God's Chosen, upon whom his blessing had been bestowed, had been cast out of Jerusalem. Because of their sin which they committed, these people would be sorely punished by sword and dispersion. In the eyes of the nations the people of Judah and their God had suffered disastrous defeat. Since God's ultimate purpose through Judah and Israel or through life and history was to reveal his "holy name" (that is, his real Person and true purpose), this misinterpretation thwarted his ultimate concern. In very human terms Ezekiel explains that the Almighty was embarrassed by the false interpretations put on recent events among the nations.

God's ultimate purpose in the restoration of his Chosen People was the revelation of himself to all people. In the eyes of the nations God's holy and gracious name will be honored when he cleanses his people and restores them to their land (vss. 22-25).

Ezekiel, like Jeremiah before him, understood that a real change in the life of a person or a people had to begin at the motive center of personality; so he predicates the ideal future on a basic change in human nature. "A new heart I will give you, and a new spirit I will put within you; and I will take out of your flesh the heart of stone and give you a heart of flesh" (vs. 26). Verse 28 re-establishes the terms of the Covenant for a cleansed and renewed people. The land will experience great abundance, and the suffering of famine will no longer be in the land. In this new situation the restored people will remember their past sins and abominations with loathing. This is all done that the name of the Lord (his character and purpose) may be known among the nations of the world, because under such circumstances people who heretofore had doubted the reality of God would change their way of speaking. Witnessing the mercy of the Lord toward an unworthy people, the nations would exclaim, "This land that was desolate has become like the garden of Eden . . . and ruined cities are now inhabited and fortified" (vs. 35). Such evidence is incontrovertible even when given to pagan nations.

Verses 37 and 38 form a footnote on restoration. There will not be a token restoration; rather, the land will be fully populated. The figure of the "flock" seems to be a repetition of the ideas of chapter 34, where these verses were probably originally found. Editorial rearrangement accounts for their dislocation.

Vision of Dry Bones (37:1-28)

Two real-life problems which grew out of the Exile are met in this chapter. First, Judah was like a dead nation without future, bereft of hope. Second, the tragic rupture between Judah and Israel had not been healed but remained historically existent. These two problems form the background for chapter 37.

Like many of Ezekiel's visions, it is possible that this one is a subconscious reflection of a conscious experience. He probably had seen on occasion the dry bones of those who, having fallen in battle, were left unburied. In vision he saw all of Judah and Jerusalem in the state of hopeless death. The Lord asks his prophet the perplexing question, "Son of man, can these bones live?" Ezekiel answers, "O Lord GOD, thou knowest." Only God could answer the question because in his hands alone are the powers of life and death.

Afterward the Almighty commands the prophet to prophesy over these bones and promises that he will reclothe them with flesh and give them breath. Man at creation, according to the Hebrew account, became a "living being" (truly man) when the "breath" of God was breathed into him. Until that moment man was an inert body fashioned from the dust of the earth. To Ezekiel the difference between true life and actual death was possession of God's "breath" or "spirit."

In response to God's command Ezekiel spoke the word of God. The Hebrews thought of God's word as a creative agent working through his prophet. The word was more than a sound disturbing the tranquillity of the air; it carried with it the full power of the speaker. So God's creative word re-created life where death had been. As the prophet spoke, the Spirit ("breath") of God possessed dry bones, making them into a mighty army (vss. 7-10). Life is meaningless existence until it is given meaning by the indwelling Spirit of God.

Ezekiel now relates the vision to a life situation, as must any prophet of God. "Our bones are dried up, and our hope is lost; we are clean cut off," was a byword at that time (vs. 11b). God promises to open the graves of those who have died and make them live. This is not to be taken as a promise of general resurrection of the dead; on the contrary, it relates to those for whom existence has become for all intents and purposes a grave. To such folk who are now in the grave of exile the Almighty promises, "And I will put my Spirit within you, and you shall live, and I will place you in your own land" (vs. 14a).

In verses 15-23 there is a subsequent command from God to the prophet. He is to take two sticks; upon one he is to write the name "Judah" (the Southern Kingdom), and upon the other he is to write the name "Joseph" (Israel, or the Northern Kingdom). Then in dramatic act the prophet joins the sticks together as God commands him to do. Following the dramatic act, which probably took place before an audience in a public place, Ezekiel explains its meaning. Here is the same sequence of act and interpretation found in other parts of the book. Reunion of the disrupted kingdom of David is promised. The tragedy of separation had continued across the years with little hope for healing. Israel's inhabitants had faded into the unnumbered and nameless multitudes of the earth or had become part of half-breed Samaria. But now God promises that the exiles of North and South shall be brought to their homeland, where once more one King shall rule over them. In this reunited land the old defilements and abominations shall no longer rise to bring disaster.

In a reunited kingdom, only one person could possibly rule and that would be David, who historically had created the kingdom (vss. 24-28). His, not Solomon's, was the Golden Age which became a pattern for future hope. David, who has been previously identified as God's shepherd over Israel, is once more so designated. Under his rule ordinances will be kept and statutes obeyed. The people will come back to the land once given to Jacob, the common father of both Israel and Judah—a reminder that the land belonged to them together. An everlasting Covenant of peace will be established with this restored and reunited people. The ideal Covenant relation is expressed as the prophet, speaking for God, says, "My dwelling place shall be with them; and I will be their God, and they shall be my people" (vs. 27).

Gog and Magog (38:1—39:29)

Chronologically these two chapters, the repetitiousness of which suggests a combination of several sources, belong after the restoration of Israel in the land of Palestine in the security and peace of God's Covenant of peace. Whether or not the section as a whole comes originally from the hand of the prophet Ezekiel is problematical and is a matter of considerable current debate. Its ideas belong to the historical period out of which Ezekiel spoke, and there is a high degree of probability that it is shaped by his spirit and thought, if indeed it was not written by his hand.

A restored people in a physical land of Palestine could never be safe so long as the menace of invasion remained on the horizon. Ezekiel, therefore, foresaw the time when God would win his final, cosmic victory by overcoming those forces from the ends of the earth which would rise up against him and his people Israel.

Obviously the last paragraph of the section (39:25-29)—which predicts the return of Judah from captivity, an event presupposed in 38:1—39:24—is out of its proper chronological order. This paragraph should be understood as a separate fragment which the editors of the book placed in this spot for reasons which now elude us.

Vision and Prophecy Concerning Gog (38:1-9)

Identification of Gog with a historical figure has been attempted often but with very little success. Neither Gog nor the cryptic land of Magog appears to fit any known historical figure or political power existent at the time. Gog therefore should be understood in symbolic terms as the very epitome of evil in history. Darkness and light are in a tense struggle on the stage of history. Ezekiel pictures the battle now reaching a climax when the final victory is to be won. This immense concept must not be lost because the format for its expression is so literalistic.

Gog comes out of the north whence so many terrors had threatened the land of Palestine. From the north invaders had come with stunning and deadly regularity. The names "Meshech" and "Tubal," which also appear in Genesis 10, can be identified with two cities in southern Asia Minor. Persia was the horizon of the ancient world looking toward Asia; Cush is to be identified with Ethiopia; and Put is located on the North African shoreline where Libya is today. Gomer means Cimmerians, while Beth-togormah was a location on the Black Sea in the north. All these places are listed in the Genesis table of nations and represent the ends of the earth as Ezekiel knew the earth. These will all be gathered together with Gog from the land of Magog. It goes without saying that the names of these ancient places do not contain any reference to modern nations and states.

Gog and his allied host will descend upon the restored land of Israel, which is living securely in peace (vss. 7-8). The advance of this great multitude from the ends of the earth will be so tremendous that it can be most accurately likened to a storm covering the landscape (vs. 9). So the scene is set and the characters are on stage.

Gog's Plot (38:10-13)

That the opportunity for easy conquest is almost irresistible to the chief culprit is revealed by his words, "I will go up against the land of unwalled villages; I will fall upon the quiet people who dwell securely, all of them dwelling without walls, and having no bars or gates" (vs. 11). Hunger for conquest has seldom been stopped by high motives; it has been deterred by walls and by the threat of defeat. Neither hindrance was a problem for Gog. These peaceful folk stood helpless before his onslaught. With him he now gathers cohorts from Sheba (the southern Arabian peninsula) and Dedan (located on the northern end of the same land mass). Merchants from Tarshish, which is either in Spain or in Sardinia, also join the great army. Their primary motive is the economic one, frequently at the base of conquest whatever its rationalization or justification. Thus in the figure of "Gog" the Lord is meeting head on those forces in history which make for chaos rather than order, for evil rather than good.

The Great Battle (38:14-23)

The Lord proclaims that *he* will bring Gog against the land. The decision has not been made by Gog but by the Lord, who has himself brought on this crisis. The reason for God's action is the same one that runs through most of the book. By the defeat of Gog, the Lord says, "I vindicate my holiness before their eyes."

Verse 17 makes reference to the fact, which must have been known to the readers, that God's prophets had long looked forward to this climactic victory over Gog. When the day comes, the Lord himself will take charge. The earth will shake, mountains will be thrown down, and walls will all be flattened. The Lord is opposing Gog not through an army but directly by earthquake (vss. 19-20). In the resulting confusion the forces of Gog will fight among themselves. Pestilence, heavy rains, fire, and brimstone will be used to finish the destruction. By entering thus directly into a final historical cataclysmic event, God makes complete his victory.

Overthrow and Defeat of Gog (39:1-10)

Verses 1-6 repeat much that has already been said in the previous chapter. Gog, the chief prince of Meshech and Tubal, will come out of the north against the cities of Israel. Destruction of Gog will be complete, leaving him and his hosts as prey for vultures. Consuming fire from heaven will descend upon Gog and upon the coastlands.

Verses 7-8 repeat the thought that the destruction of Gog is accomplished so that God's holy name shall no longer be profaned before the nations. Seeing what has happened in this final debacle of evil, they shall know that God is "the LORD, the Holy One in Israel."

The extent of desolation and defeat is detailed in verses 9-10, where it is said that the accumulated weapons are so great in quantity that it takes seven years for fire to consume them. So great is the junk yard of weapons that there will need to be no wood cut for fuel or for cooking over a seven-year period.

Burial and Disposal of Gog's Army (39:11-20)

Gog and his hosts appear to be trapped in a valley whence there is no escape. There they are buried on the spot in the valley called "Hamon-gog," which is "the multitude of Gog." In order that the land of Israel be not defiled by the dead bodies, men are appointed to bury them. Working continuously they spend seven months on the burial. The use of "seven years" (vs. 9) and "seven months" (vs. 12) indicates that this whole account was symbolic from its inception.

After burial of the bodies there follows a feast at which the birds and beasts consume the mighty who have fallen (vss. 17-20).

Had the interment already occurred, there would be no corpses upon which to feed. These verses must therefore be understood as a separate oracle which has been brought into the complex of chapters 38-39 without logical connection.

Israel's Return from Captivity (39:21-29)

The earlier motif combining explanation of judgment with promise of restoration is repeated. Israel and all nations shall know who God is (vss. 21-22). These two verses are obviously the bridge between the Gog-Magog passage and the remainder of this chapter. The reason for Israel's captivity will be understood: The Lord hid his face because of the uncleanness and transgression of his people, who refused to be his people. National destruction was no manifestation of the Lord's weakness; it was the sin of Israel which brought disaster.

Restored Israel, located where none will "make them afraid," is described once more. After return and settlement of the people in the land, the Lord promises that he will pour out his Spirit upon the people (see ch. 37). The picture of Israel restored in a world where no enemy can hurt is an emerging promise in Scripture. God will give security by ultimately winning the victory over chaos and darkness through order and light. In this pattern of thought the basic struggle of life and history is carefully and dramatically described.

THE TEMPLE AND THE CITY OF GOD
Ezekiel 40:1—48:35

This last large section of the book has caused more controversy than any other, except perhaps chapters 38-39. Many interpreters deny that the section in its entirety belongs to the prophet of the Chaldean Captivity. That, it would seem, is going much too far, although there is possibly more editorial material combined with Ezekiel's thought here than elsewhere. It is to be doubted that 43:13-27, a detailed description of the altar of burnt offering and its ritual, is original; however, it is a necessary consequence, albeit later, of the prophet's thought. The detailed rules for priests (44: 25-27, 31) and a portion of 45:1—46:18 can hardly be considered parts of the prophet's original masterpiece. Whether or not 47:13 —48:35 belongs to Ezekiel is a problem; we believe it came from his hand either directly or through his disciples.

Measurement of the Temple (40:1—42:20)

Central to any restoration was the Temple, but the Temple apart from the presence of God would be useless. The prophet sees the Temple in some detail and then meets the Lord himself in the midst thereof. The date for this vision of the Temple fits into the same system as all the other dates in the book, this one being specifically the twenty-fifth anniversary of destruction and exile. Ezekiel is transported to the Holy Land in a visionary visit as he had been on previous occasions (chs. 8 and 11) and is perched atop a high mountain near the city, possibly the Mount of Olives. The heavenly figure who appears at that spot is probably the same figure as the one described in chapters 8 and 9, but now his task is construction, not destruction. His linen clothes identify him with the Temple, whose priests wore linen clothes. The prophet is told to listen and watch carefully because what he is about to witness is of immense importance.

Details of the Temple begin with measurement and description of the East Gate of the outer wall according to a typical gate plan. The form dates from the tenth century B.C. The outside walls form an over-all structure of 500 x 500 cubits. Then within that area stand the inner walls of the Temple area itself; these walls, like the outer walls, have three separate gates. Thus there are two gates on each of the three sides—north, south, and east—one in the outer wall and one in the inner wall nearest the Temple. The pavement and the outer court are between the two sets of walls. This description is a reflection of the dimensions of the East Gate in Solomon's Temple. After the prophet has seen the measurement of the outer East Gate, he sees the outer court and pavement with thirty chambers built next to the outer wall, and with the pavement running around inside the wall. From the inner to the outer gate is 100 cubits (vss. 17-19).

The outer North Gate, like the East Gate, is described as separated by 100 cubits from the matching inner North Gate. Like the other, this gate has an over-all measurement of 50 x 25 cubits, and it has seven steps leading up to the vestibule (vss. 20-23). A description of an identical set of South Gates follows, being 100 cubits distant from each other. It should be understood that there was no West Gate; the Temple faced toward the east and had no rear entrance (vss. 24-31).

Having described in some detail the structure of the gates on the outer wall, the prophet now describes the corresponding gates on the inner wall which is within the outer wall. The South, East, and North Gates are all measured and found to be identical with the outer gates in measurement (that is, 50 x 25 cubits) but have eight steps instead of seven leading to the vestibule (vss. 32-37).

A chamber on one side of the vestibule of the inner North Gate is used for washing the offerings, and two tables on either side are provided for the actual slaughter of sacrificial animals. There are four tables in the vestibule, and apparently four are provided outside the wall at the bottom of the steps leading from the outer court to the vestibule. In addition, four stone tables are provided as a storage surface for the sacrificial slaughter instruments (vss. 38-43).

Within the inner court, beside the North and South Gates respectively, there were matching rooms provided as dressing rooms for Temple personnel. The room near the North Gate is for the priests who have charge of the altar, that is to say, "the sons of Zadok." They alone among the sons of Levi have the right to come near to the Lord in service at the altar. The inner court which leads immediately to the Temple door measures 100 x 100 cubits and is the location for the altar of the Temple (40:44-47). Moving in good order the prophet and his guide now reach the Temple entrance itself which is, of course, smaller than the other gateways, measuring fourteen cubits, with ten steps leading into the vestibule. The vestibule itself measures 20 x 12 cubits, with ten steps leading into it from the outer court. On either side of the entrance are free-standing pillars (40:48-49). As the prophet comes into the nave of the Temple, its inner dimensions of 40 x 20 cubits are measured. The entrance to the nave is said to be ten cubits wide, with jambs on each side of six cubits in breadth (41:1-2). Finally, the prophet enters "the most holy place," which measures 20 x 20 cubits (vss. 3-4).

The Temple wall is six cubits thick, and side chambers along the wall are four cubits wide. Thus the sanctuary had double walls with four cubits between them where the service rooms were built on three stories. Room for these chambers was larger the higher the wall went, because as the wall grew thinner, space for rooms was increased. The outer wall of these side chambers was five cubits thick, one cubit less than the Temple wall itself. The paving or platform on which the Temple rested was twenty cubits broad all around the Temple. Doors into these rooms between the walls were located on the north and south walls of the Temple and were five cubits wide (vss. 5-11).

The building behind the Temple facing west where there is no inner gate measures 70 x 90 cubits (vs. 12). The Temple and its immediate area made a perfect square, including open yard on three sides, and including the vestibule, nave, and Most Holy Place in the over-all length (vss. 13-15a).

Having finished a general description of the Temple, the prophet, drawing on his visionary visit, gives details of the interior decorations of the nave. The walls are paneled, and upon them are carvings of cherubim and palm trees alternately (vss. 15b-20). Just in front of "the holy place" an altar or table of wood is seen which is described by the guide in these words: "This is the table which is before the LORD." Both the nave and the Holy Place are entered by double swinging doors. On the doors, as on the walls, the decor consists of carved cherubim and palm trees.

Chapter 42, though not completely clear, deals with two buildings which flank the Temple on either side (north and south); these measure 100 x 50 cubits and like the walls are three stories in height. Details of the structures are somewhat confusing, as is the use to which these large buildings are to be put. Rooms facing out toward the outer wall are one hundred cubits long while rooms facing the inner court are but fifty cubits. Apparently the rooms are to be twenty cubits wide, with a passageway ten cubits wide running between them. However, the author explains that the upper rooms are not as wide as the lower, since part of the breadth is used for balconies or galleries (42:1-10a).

In addition to these two service buildings, two more rooms on the south against the inner wall are described. In these four rooms the priests consume the holy offerings (the cereal offering, the sin offering, and the guilt offering). Since the Temple and the priestly garments are dedicated, the garments will be stored here lest they be contaminated when the priests go into the outer court (vss. 10b-14).

Finally, the entire structure (the dimensions of the outer wall) is measured and is found to be 500 x 500 cubits. In these terms Ezekiel foresaw the rebuilt Temple of the future, God's sanctuary established and operative for the honor of God in the midst of a restored and renewed people.

Appearance of the Glory of the Lord (43:1-12)

The Lord, whose departure from the city was the signal for its destruction and the destruction of the Temple in its midst, now returns to the restored Temple via the East Gate whence he had left (10:18-19; 11:22-23). Ezekiel explains that his vision is the same which he saw at Chebar on the occasion before the city fell. The Spirit of the Lord lifts the prophet up and brings him to the inner court within the East Gate (vs. 5).

God now sets forth the conditions for his return: "Now let them put away their idolatry and the dead bodies of their kings far from me, and I will dwell in their midst for ever" (vs. 9).

God's commission to Ezekiel is a simple one: to describe the Temple structure and its operating functions. When the people are willing to submit to God, it will be restored. Shame will lead them to repentance (vss. 10-12). Now that the glory of the Lord rests once more in the Temple, making it again the place of meeting between God and Israel, the promise of restoration is given a new dimension.

Regulations for the Temple Service (43:13—46:24)

The Altar and Its Use (43:13-27)

The altar consists of a series of platforms placed one on the other, with the hearth at the top measuring 12 x 12 cubits. The steps are facing eastward, as is the front door of the Temple.

On this altar the sons of Zadok will make burnt offerings to God. Procedure for sacrifice during eight days of atonement ritual is listed, paralleling the account in Exodus (Exod. 29:35-37). Seven days are set aside for consecration of the altar itself, culminating with burnt offerings and peace offerings being made for the people, "from the eighth day onward."

Personnel of the Temple (44:1—45:12)

Coming to the East Gate the prophet finds it closed because the Lord has sanctified it by entering the city through it. It will remain permanently closed; only the prince may enter, and that by way of the vestibule.

Ezekiel is told to listen carefully so that he may know who will be admitted to the Temple and who must be excluded from it (vss. 4-8). Much of the immediate past tragedy is explained by the willingness of Israel to allow pagan influences in the Temple. Foreigners are to be positively excluded henceforth. This exclusivist attitude came into great prominence in the age of Nehemiah and Ezra, leading finally to the ingrown quality of Jewish religion in the time of Jesus.

The Levitical priests are blamed for worshiping idols and participating in the abominations which led to the destruction of Israel (vss. 9-14). Hereafter the Levites will not share with the sons of Zadok as priests but will do the menial tasks necessary to the operation of the Temple, such as keeping the gate and preparing sacrifice. This is in all probability a natural consequence and permanent result of an earlier reform which had centralized worship in Jerusalem and which had designated the Zadokites as the only priests.

In keeping with this pattern the functions of the priesthood are forthwith assigned to "the sons of Zadok" (vs. 15). Certain behavior and requirements are laid upon those who will serve before the Lord's altar. A priest is not to shave his head, nor marry a widow, nor drink wine before a service (vss. 20-22). The functions of the priests extend beyond narrowly sacerdotal activity before the altar. The priests are to distinguish the common from the holy, decide controversies between people, keep all the laws of God, and reverence the Sabbath (vss. 23-24). In other words, in the restored Temple they are to combine functions of priest, prophet, and judge. A priest may not go near a human corpse, except when the deceased has been a member of his immediate family. Then he must afterward undergo seven days of ritual cleansing and upon entering the inner court make a sin offering for himself. The Zadokites are thus given the holiest responsibilities in restored Israel.

The priests will have no inheritance of their own because God is "their inheritance." They are assigned the following provisions to eat: the cereal offering, the sin offering, and the guilt offering. Every devoted thing shall, in the name of the Lord, belong to the priests, as shall the first fruits of all things. In addition, the first of "coarse meal" is assigned to them, but the priests may not eat any bird or animal which has died naturally or has been killed accidentally (vss. 28-31).

As if the above apportionment were not large enough, God assigns a block of territory in the midst of the land, 25,000 x

25,000 cubits, which will belong to the sons of Zadok. In one section, 25,000 x 10,000 cubits, the Temple is to be located, surrounded by a strip of "no man's land." The priests will have the Temple section as their dwelling place. Another section of equal size, 25,000 x 10,000 cubits, will be set aside for the Levitical Temple servants. The remaining 25,000 x 5,000 cubit area will belong to the whole house of Israel as a unit, rather than being divided among the tribes (45:1-6). The prince will own property on both sides of the holy district to the east and the west, extending all the way to the eastern and western frontiers. This generous provision will keep the prince from being tempted to seek gain by oppression (vss. 7-8).

After the assignment of territory to the prince, two exhortations to future rulers are made, each touched with the prophetic fire typical of Ezekiel in his earlier oracles (vss. 9-12). Princes are urged to put away violence and oppression, and to base their policies rather on justice and righteousness. In terms similar to those used by Amos and Isaiah, the princes are urged to cease evicting people from their land. Princes and kings, having no property, had often, like Ahab, taken what they wanted, although God had sent his prophets to denounce and judge this very kind of rule. Moreover, kings and princes had been known to change weights and measures to their advantage. The prince is now told to set and make standard all weights and measures.

Instructions for Sacrifice (45:13—46:24)

This major section describes the amounts of the offerings which the prince is to receive from the people and to offer to God (vss. 13-17). Verses 18-20 deal with atonement for, or dedication of, the Temple.

The Feast of the Passover is described with detailed instructions concerning the amounts of offerings to be made by the prince (45:21-25). For seven days unleavened bread shall be eaten. On the seven days of celebration seven young bulls and seven rams shall be offered, together with a he-goat, as a sin offering. Cereal and oil offerings are also to be made. At the Feast of Tabernacles the same offerings shall be repeated (vs. 25). These instructions are at variance with those recorded in Numbers and elsewhere, proving that the cultic practice of a dynamic faith changes with time.

A relatively long discussion of Sabbaths and new moons is

given by the prophet. Again we find that the East Gate is closed, except on the Sabbath and the new moon, when it is to be opened that the prince may enter by the vestibule and take his stand there. Details of the offerings to be made on stated occasions follow (46:1-8). Procedure for entering the Temple area is then given. A man must not leave by the gate through which he entered, and the worshiping group is to be accompanied by the prince (vss. 9-10). Details of offerings which the prince will make are described, and the procedure for offering is given (vss. 11-15).

A rule for holding property in perpetuity reflects the sad chronicle of Israelite history in which the Year of Jubilee had never been actively observed (see Lev. 25). When the prince makes a gift to his sons out of his inheritance, the property is a permanent inheritance of the sons and their heirs. On the other hand, when the prince donates some of his property to a servant, it shall remain in the keeping of the servant until the "year of liberty," probably every seventh year, and then return to the prince. Thus provision was made for a redistribution of the property but not on so extensive a scale as the Year of Jubilee required. Since the prince possessed his own inheritance, he was forbidden to take inheritance of the common people: "None of my people shall be dispossessed of his property" (vs. 18). Historical abuses of the property rights of the people by the kings, as evidenced in Amos, Isaiah, and Micah, showed the necessity for this safeguard in Ezekiel's vision of the future.

The narrative continues, describing in the western side of the inner court some kind of enclosure where the priests boiled the guilt offering and the sin offering and where they also baked the cereal offering. This was a kitchen where the priests prepared the offering which was theirs exclusively to eat before God (vss. 19-20). In the outer court at the four corners within the walls there were four smaller courts, 40 x 30 cubits, equipped with hearths for cooking. These were the kitchens where the Levites prepared portions of the sacrifices of which it was the privilege and the duty of the people to partake (vss. 21-24).

Healing Waters (47:1-12)

Ezekiel now depicts the influence of the re-established Temple and its effect upon the land. Coming to the back of the Temple the prophet sees a stream of water issuing from the threshold of the Temple and coming out on the south side of the Temple. Going to the outside of the sanctuary area, he sees the stream flowing outward. The same heavenly figure who has been companion to the prophet through this visionary visit to the restored city is still beside Ezekiel with a measuring line in his hand. One thousand cubits from the Temple the water was ankle-deep, and thereafter it grew progressively deeper as it flowed farther from the Temple. Finally, as it went eastward toward the Dead Sea, the stream became a mighty river in an otherwise desolate and barren land (vss. 1-6).

Standing on the bank of this River of God the prophet witnesses a remarkable transformation in the landscape, which had been the most barren and useless area of Palestine, as it is to this day. This water moving southward by way of the Arabah, the great geologic depression in the south, entered the Dead Sea with its brackish waters and caused the deadly waters to become fresh. In these renewed waters there will be many fish, so that fishermen will stand by the shore from En-gedi to En-eglaim (two small springs in an otherwise desolate shore line). The fish will be of many kinds, like those found in the Mediterranean. Yet nature will keep her balance. Swamps and marshes will retain their saline content lest this essential substance be totally removed. On the banks of the river, fruit trees will flourish, bearing fruit each month and having luxuriant leaves. The fruit will be for food and the leaves for medicinal purposes. The transformation is possible because water has issued from the Temple of God to transform a desert and make it into a garden. God's presence alone makes the desert blossom like a rose. Those familiar with the Book of Revelation will recognize in this life-giving stream the pattern for the same figure in the last book of the Bible (see Rev. 22:1-2).

Division of the Restored Land (47:13—48:35)

The restored land is given back into the hands of the twelve tribes, with two portions going to the house of Joseph—Ephraim and Manasseh (47:13-14). Four boundaries are set for the whole new land in which the restored and reunited kingdom will dwell in peace (47:15-20). Then the division of the land is ordered, with provision for aliens who settle in the land to be treated as native-born sons of Israel (47:21—48:35).

Beginning with the northern border and proceeding south to the area reserved for the city, the Temple, and the prince, seven divisions are made in this order: Dan, Asher, Naphtali, Manasseh, Ephraim, Reuben, and Judah. This is artificial and idealized division and has little if any connection with historic reality, past or present. Divisions and boundary lines completely ignore historic and geographical factors, since both were unimportant for the purposes of this oracle.

In the midst of the land, just south of the inheritance of Judah, there shall be established the holy district, 25,000 x 25,000 cubits. The priests are to be allotted 25,000 x 10,000 cubits (48:9, margin), in which they will live and where the Temple will be located, and the Levites are to be given the same-sized tract for their own needs (compare 44:28—45:8). None of this consecrated territory may under any conditions be sold or even temporarily exchanged (48:8-14). The third portion of 25,000 x 5,000 cubits is to be reserved for the use of all Israel. In the midst of the area a city 4,500 x 4,500 cubits square shall be erected, and around the city on all sides shall be a strip of land 250 cubits wide. The remaining part of the area on the east and west, two tracts 10,000 x 5,000 cubits, shall be used for the workers of the city to produce food (48:15-20).

The territory east and west of the "holy portion," and extending to the borders of the land, shall belong to the prince. This land of the prince, divided by the holy portion in the middle, is to lie between the territories of Judah and Benjamin.

In verses 23-29 the remaining tribes are given their inheritance in the restored and renewed land. Moving from the south border of the holy portion southward the allotments are in the following order: Benjamin, Simeon, Issachar, Zebulun, and Gad.

The city with measurements as previously given will have twelve gates, one for each tribe but with this significant difference: Joseph is given but one gate (not two for his sons Ephraim and Manasseh), and Levi is given a gate in this list. The city measures 18,000 cubits around and its name is "The LORD is there." The message of the entire Book of Ezekiel is given real emphasis and stress in the name bestowed upon the City of God. Destruction came in the past because the Lord was not "there"; he had withdrawn his presence from the sinful city. Future hope rests now on the promise that "The LORD is there."

THE BOOK OF

DANIEL

———

INTRODUCTION

The Book Itself

The Book of Daniel is one of the best known and yet one of the least understood books in the Bible. Its stories were learned in and are remembered from childhood, and their drama still captures our minds and grips our attention. Clear as the stories appear to be, the other material, including the visions recorded in chapters 7-12, is not so easily understood.

The structure and language of this remarkable book are by no means simple. One section is *about* Daniel (chs. 1-6) while the other is said to be *by* Daniel (chs. 7-12). To add to the confusion, there are two other divisions in the book which do not coincide with the division of stories and visions. The book itself is written in two languages: Aramaic (2:4b—7:28) and Hebrew (1:1—2:3; 8:1—12:13). No completely satisfactory explanation of this linguistic shift has been offered to date, though many explanations have been put forward. Daniel is a book divided by inconsistencies in style, language, and literary form; yet these differences do not coincide with one another.

Obviously Daniel is a composite work which has drawn on several sources. Chapter 1 was probably written on the basis of a well-known story as an introduction by the author and then was followed by popular stories which were used for a particular purpose. Chapter 7, an independent piece, binds chapters 1-6 to chapters 8-12. Whether the original language was Hebrew or Aramaic is a debatable point, although our conclusion is that it was Hebrew. Whatever its sources and its language, the book came into its present form by means of the efforts of one author and compiler. It is a single work as it now stands, although a fabric of many strands.

Date and Authorship

Traditionally the Book of Daniel has been dated in the Chaldean period during the reign of Nebuchadnezzar (605-562 B.C.) and following. Yet there are many evidences which contest this position.

On the surface it seems obvious that this book is what it purports to be: the memoirs of a Hebrew hero who lived in trying times and who had visions of a better day. Yet the reader upon closer study is introduced to the strange spectacle of a man living in one age about which he has the most sketchy knowledge, speaking not at all to his own time but speaking rather to an age 400 years in the future about which he has detailed and accurate information. That it is possible for God to inspire a man to thrust himself into the future we would not deny, but that such a projection is the basis for the Book of Daniel we would indeed question.

The alternative to the traditional date is to recognize Daniel in its present form as a book written at the beginning of the Maccabean period (about 168-165 B.C.), which was a time of terror, trial, and tragic persecution. This age is described firsthand from the point of view of the persecuted in the Intertestament book of First Maccabees.

Evidence for this date is almost overwhelming. As has been stated already, the author of Daniel possessed an incredibly accurate knowledge of the third and second centuries B.C. but had only a loose grasp of the historical situation in the sixth century B.C. The ethnic term "Chaldean" is used repeatedly (for example, in 2:2, 10; 4:7; 5:7, 11) to refer to professional wise men, not to a race or to a nation. In the era of Nebuchadnezzar, a Chaldean was a citizen of the Chaldean, or neo-Babylonian, Empire. It was centuries later that the Greeks came to use the term to describe wise men and interpreters of dreams. Thus Daniel's use of the term points away from a sixth-century date and is striking evidence for a second-century setting.

Moreover, Nebuchadnezzar did not take Jerusalem in the third year of Jehoiakim, but captured the city much later, in 598 B.C., a date which the author has confused with another date. In his third year Jehoiakim did transfer his allegiance to Nebuchadnezzar, but Jerusalem was not captured until after the Jewish king's death (see II Kings 24:1-6, 10-15).

"Darius the Mede" (Dan. 5:31) is an unidentifiable person in the Medo-Persian period and therefore must be explained as having been created by a combination of fact and imagination. Doubtless Darius the Great, a Persian emperor, was the personage whom the author had in mind, but he ruled after, not before, Cyrus the Great. In any case, he was not a Mede.

The underlying assumption of the book is that the chronological order of empires was Chaldean, Median, Persian, and Greek. Actually, however, the Chaldean and Median empires were parallel empires from 625 B.C. onward. Cyaxares the Mede assisted in the destruction of the Assyrian Empire and cleared the way for Chaldean ascendancy under Nebuchadnezzar's leadership. Apparently Median rulers continued to enjoy some semblance of autonomy during the short-lived Chaldean Empire. But when Cyrus ascended the throne of Babylon in 539 B.C., Median power was nonexistent except as an integral part of the Persian conquest and rule. There is no chronological place for a Median Empire between the Chaldean and the Persian, yet the author assumes that there was such a time of separate world empire for the Medes. It is largely because of this historical misunderstanding that "Darius the Mede" is regarded as the successor to Belshazzar the Chaldean, whose capital he destroyed according to Daniel 5, whereas in historical fact Cyrus succeeded Belshazzar.

Other evidence against a sixth-century date is plentiful. The stylized reports of the conversion of Nebuchadnezzar on several occasions (2:46-49; 4:34-37) and of Darius (6:25-27) create a picture that would hardly have been made in an age when the activities of these men gave little evidence that they had become genuine worshipers of the Lord. Later such a philosophy of history would have depended for its effectiveness not on exact historical accuracy but rather on the faith which validated it.

Having noted the author's divergence from certain known facts of history, we must take care to note also that there are some quite accurate bits of information from the Chaldean period. For example, the author knew that Nebuchadnezzar was the builder of Babylon, a fact forgotten until recent archaeological investigations recovered it. Moreover, the historicity of Belshazzar as the *de facto* king in the absence of his father Nabonidus has been substantiated by extrabiblical evidence. Nabonidus apparently spent much of his later years in the desert at Tema pursuing scholarly interests, which held greater fascination for him than did the throne. The account of Belshazzar as king, understood in this sense, squares with authentic historical data from other sources.

Writing in 200 B.C., the author of the apocryphal Book of Ecclesiasticus listed among the great men of Israel Isaiah, Jeremiah, Ezekiel, and the Twelve Prophets, but made no mention of Daniel. This can hardly have been an oversight. When a later Jewish writing (the Sibylline Oracles) was composed (after 140 B.C.), Daniel was a well-known figure. Largely because of the knowledge that Daniel was not, strictly speaking, a prophetic work, the framers of the Jewish Canon placed this book with Psalms, Proverbs, and other books in the collection known as "the Writings."

Practically all interpreters agree that Daniel speaks to the age of the Syrian ruler Antiochus IV (Epiphanes), whose rule began in 175 B.C., and that the atmosphere of this period is especially appropriate for chapters 7-12. It is obvious that the author of chapter 7 is using the four-kingdom idea as an approach to the center of his interest. The "little horn" in chapter 8 is Antiochus. Furthermore, the same point of denunciation is quickly reached in chapter 8 after the explanation of the Ram and He-Goat vision. The writer loses little time getting to the subject of central concern to himself and his readers. Moreover, chapter 11 is a remarkable and accurate narration of Seleucid and Ptolomaic history in the third and second centuries B.C.

Thus we conclude that the Book of Daniel, as it now stands, was written between 168 and 165 B.C., but that it doubtless drew on earlier sources for much of the material it contains.

The writer borrows from many sources for the full make-up of his central character. It should not pass unnoticed that as a dreamer and interpreter of dreams Daniel is very similar to Joseph, and that the course of his life at times is almost a copy of this ancestor of the Chosen People. Along with these influences the great figure of a certain "Dan'el," remembered for his wisdom throughout the Near East, must be listed as a source of the Daniel image. An amalgamation of these sources was poured into a new mold to create "Daniel," representing the truest and best of Israel.

Actually, however, the touches of historical accuracy from the Chaldean period give some basis for the conclusion that Daniel was a person who lived in that period and around whom certain legends had grown up. To be sure, this person, like David, became greater as a symbol than he ever could have been as a historical personality. He became the one who under God's guidance saw the future clearly and who enunciated the essential faith that the Almighty would ultimately be victorious in history.

The author was a person inspired of God, living under duress of persecution, who drew from the past and created a great hero-image which inspired the weak to be strong. Having established the hero, through his lips the author speaks that message of hope which God gave to a troubled day. The name "Daniel" itself is perhaps not to be overlooked since it means "God judges." What the author's name or general identity was we do not know. In any case, he used a variety of materials and was influenced by the ideas of many, but it was the stamp of his experience and genius, under God, which made the book one of the truly great theological treatises of all time.

Historical Background

The actual historical background for the Book of Daniel must start with the reign of Alexander the Great (336-323 B.C.), a student of the great philosopher Aristotle, a brilliant military strategist, and a zealous disciple and exponent of Hellenistic (Greek) culture. In 334 B.C. he began the conquest of Asia Minor and the Middle East, and after two years most of the area was under his rule. With this conquest came a way of life including Greek thought, language, manners, morals, and religion. Alexander was never satisfied with physical conquest; he dreamed of one world drawn together under the "enlightened and superior" Greek way of life. Both military conquest and cultural intrusion were welcomed by some people in Palestine, but for others they were evil forces which must be resisted to the death (see I Macc. 1:10-64).

When Alexander died in 323 B.C., Hellenism had already made a permanent impression on the Middle East. Greek was spoken everywhere. Stadia had been built in many cities and seasonal Greek games were held. Greek clothing was worn and Greek manners were imitated. In fact, the Hellenistic spirit exercised a major influence on religious ideas and values.

At Alexander's death, there being no heir to the throne, succession became a matter for contest. After long struggle and much intrigue, four of the late emperor's generals divided the empire among themselves. The spheres of their power were centered respectively in Greece, Asia Minor, Syro-Mesopotamia, and Egypt. For our purposes the Syro-Mesopotamian and Egyptian regions are most important, because it was in these regions that the Greek way clashed most violently with Jewish faith and life.

In Syria, Seleucus took power, bestowing his name upon the Seleucid dynasty, while in Egypt Ptolemy ruled, attaching his name to the Ptolemaic dynasty which he founded. Between these two centers of political power, Palestine became again a land bridge for commerce or military conquest, as it had been often since the dawn of civilization. As such it was a most desirable prize which could serve either as a foothold for conquest or as a buffer against attack.

For most of the third century Palestine remained under the sovereignty of the Ptolemies, although the Seleucids were not loath to challenge Egyptian rule at every opportunity. Under Egyptian (Ptolemaic) domination the Jews were left largely free to follow their own customs and practice their own religion, as they had during the Persian era. That situation, however, began to change imperceptibly after Antiochus III established rule over Palestine following the battle of Paneas in 198 B.C. Nevertheless, no overt repression of either life or faith began until Antiochus Epiphanes ascended the throne.

Early in his reign Antiochus Epiphanes, who believed he was Zeus incarnate, agreed to sell the office of high priest to the highest bidder. No conceivable action could have struck more horror into Jewish hearts or caused greater revulsion to Jewish minds, though such a procedure was quite normal in the lands neighboring on Palestine. Onias III, the legitimate high priest, was deposed in 175 B.C. when Jason bought the office. In 171 B.C., however, a higher bid was made by Menelaus. Upon the acceptance of Menelaus' offer, Jason in his turn was deposed from office. In order to forestall any future claim, Onias was murdered. Jason, having fled into Ammonite territory, bided his time until the absence of Antiochus for a military advance along the Egyptian frontier afforded him opportunity to reimpose his power. When Antiochus returned from his unsuccessful military campaign he sacked the Temple, and Menelaus was returned to his priestly duties. These "high priests" thus embraced a liberal Judaism which made them willing to refashion their heritage into the form of Syro-Hellenistic religion.

Soon thereafter Antiochus Epiphanes turned his full attention and energy to the cultural integration of Jewish life and faith into Greek forms. This, as it turned out, was no small task. First, the royal general Apollonius took the citadel of Jerusalem and garrisoned it against counterattack. In December 168 b.c. the regular sacrifices at the Temple were discontinued in favor of the kind of worship more in accord with Hellenistic tradition. Instead of ancient, honored practice being followed, the pig—precisely the animal most despised by the Jews—was sacrificed on the holy altar. For three years the abomination continued. This period left a deep imprint on the mind of the author of Daniel and largely explains the utter contempt in which he held the Seleucid monarch. Zeus Olympus, not the Lord, was worshiped on Zion, while Zeus Xenius was the god installed at Samaria. Circumcision, Sabbath keeping, and the possession of the Torah were crimes punishable by death. Of course, regular sacrifice was forbidden (I Macc. 1:54-61). How deeply the righteous people felt about this is demonstrated in the Aramaic translation of the name "Zeus Olympus," which by slight change comes to mean "abomination of desolation."

The attitudes toward the new order were manifold. To the very devout, assimilation of the ways of the Gentiles was the ultimate tragedy, to be resisted at all costs. But for a great many sophisticated and cosmopolitan Jews, accommodation to change was equated with enlightenment and progress. To understand this attitude it is necessary to analyze the feelings of those involved. Such a reform, according to the best Hellenistic view, merely meant that there was but one high God alternately called "Zeus" or "the Lord." In this instance a world view of religion was operative. Antiochus, not understanding the Jewish mind, thought that by removing the distinctive and separatist marks of this faith (such as the Torah, circumcision, the Sabbath, and sacrifice) he could cause the Jews to identify themselves with the whole family of man.

Many Jews quickly agreed to the idea and wholeheartedly supported the program. Stadia and gymnasia were built and Greek games became quite popular. Youth was especially drawn to the games and festivals wherein old restraints were relaxed. The use of a hat with a brim, associated with the pagan deity Mercury, and the removal of the mark of circumcision by painful operation became common (I Macc. 1:14-15, 41-50).

Resistance took two forms: outright defiance and withdrawal.

Most chose the latter way. Great numbers of people moved away from heavily inhabited areas and lived out of contact with Seleucid authority (I Macc. 1:53). This raised two problems for Antiochus. First, it constituted direct defiance of a royal decree, which could not be tolerated; and, second and more important, it reduced the tax receipts from these sources since a taxpayer who could not be located could hardly be taxed.

In order to complete his cultural and religious reform Antiochus sent royal officials to various areas for the express purpose of enforcing the royal decrees. His method of assuring local acceptance was simple. An altar was built and then before the eyes of the local citizens a designated Jew was commanded to sacrifice a pig to Zeus Olympus. This program was the spark which lighted the fires of rebellion.

Rebellion began in the small village of Modein in 168 B.C. when a renegade Jew, ready to conform to the new order, stepped to the altar to make the Gentile sacrifice. At that moment Mattathias, a local priest, filled with indignation and consumed with rage, struck down the renegade Jew and the royal officer who was the king's representative (I Macc. 2:1-28). So began the Maccabean revolt, which was led initially by Mattathias until his death about a year later. At his death Judas, one of his five sons (John, Simon, Judas, Eleazar, and Jonathan), became the leader of effective guerrilla warfare against royal forces (I Macc. 2:65—3:60). He was nicknamed "Maccabeus," which possibly means "hammerer," and from the nickname the movement got its name.

It would serve no useful purpose to trace in detail the victories of Judas over the forces of Syria, since these can be followed in any competent history of the period. Victories at Beth-horon and Emmaus were followed by an inconclusive engagement at Beth-zur. Negotiations brought hostilities to an end, with freedom of all religious practices restored. Judas finally took Jerusalem, and on December 25, 164 B.C., the Temple was cleansed and reconstituted for regular worship (I Macc. 4:52-61). A year later Antiochus Epiphanes, who was popularly called Antiochus Epimanes ("the madman"), died. But the author of Daniel apparently did not live to witness that event.

The composition of the Book of Daniel is properly set at the beginning of the Maccabean revolt when persecution of the Jews was at its height and when the issue was still in considerable doubt. Two major themes of the book are appropriately struck for such an age: courage in the present and hope for the future.

Antiochus IV was the contemporary figure who was target for the bitterest denunciation in story and vision. He is the "little horn." He arose as successor to one of the four claimants to Alexander's empire as described in chapters 7 and 8. It was he who interrupted and abolished worship in the Temple for 2300 evenings and mornings (8:14), or three and a half years (7:25; 12:7), or 1290 days (12:11), or 1335 days (12:12). These numbers each represent roughly the time lapse between 168 and 165 B.C., when in fact no legitimate sacrifice was offered in the Temple. Prophetic prediction is seldom mathematically exact, so all of the above figures are to be understood as referring to the time when, by royal decree, regular sacrificial worship at the Temple was discontinued.

In this time of desperate trial for the Jewish faith there were doubtless many among the Jews who felt that God had abandoned them. Some, on the other hand, were enthralled by the attractiveness of the new way. To reinforce the abiding value of true religion and to assure the persecuted that God would have his way, this remarkable literary piece was written. It was a "tract for the times," drawn out of adversity and trial to speak God's word to that adversity and tribulation.

So that the reader may have ready access to key dates in this complicated era we list the following significant high points:

605 B.C.	Beginning of Nebuchadnezzar's reign
539 B.C.	Accession of Cyrus to throne of Babylon
323 B.C.	Death of Alexander the Great
198 B.C.	Beginning of Seleucid control of Palestine
175-163 B.C.	Reign of Antiochus Epiphanes
175-171 B.C.	Jason, high priest
171-162 B.C.	Menelaus, high priest
168 B.C.	Mattathias' revolt at Modein
167 B.C.	Leadership by Judas Maccabeus
164 B.C.	Restoration of the Temple and religious privileges

The Message of the Book

The Sovereignty of God

The sovereignty of God was not a new concept discovered by the author amid the fires of Maccabean adversity, but it was given a new dimension by this remarkable theologian. He recognized constantly that all earthly power exists only at the sufferance of the Almighty. God is sovereign over the four world empires, whose domain at best is ephemeral. It is his rule and his Kingdom alone that shall be everlasting. He can watch over youths in bondage and can extricate the righteous from fiery furnace or lions' den. His judgment drives the great to madness and brings to nought the most ostentatious king and kingdom.

God's rule and authority, which are the basis for all earthly sovereignty, will finally establish an everlasting Kingdom at an appropriate time. Daniel apparently believed that this Kingdom might immediately be established upon earth. In a spiritual sense that final Kingdom was and is being established in Jesus Christ. The intuitive and theological assertion by the Church that such is the case is quite correct, but it is not a conclusion which this writer foresaw in detail.

Conformity and Faith

The enticements of a new way of life were current in the era from which this book arose. Pagan culture in its Greek form was very attractive, and hence it presented a serious challenge to hereditary Jewish faith. The Book of Daniel served to unmask Greek cultural claims and reveal what they really were.

These stories are combined with apocalyptic visions to call men to a faith that will not conform to the latest fashion or follow the customs of the day. Under threat of the fiery furnace three men said that even if they were not released by the power of God, still they would not submit to the degradation of heathen practice. It is interesting to note that Mattathias when exhorting his followers to courage makes reference to Shadrach, Meshach, and Abednego (I Macc. 2:59). In each of the early chapters the way of loyal faith is shown to be the right way, and the visions teach that faith is the ground of assurance of God's ultimate victory.

Salvation

Daniel takes a step forward in his understanding of "salvation." To him final redemption was presaged by the individual experiences of rescue and support evidenced in the first six chapters. This view was not new to the Israelite mind. The Kingdom of God, however, which shall intrude into history replacing all other kingdoms (the four kingdoms), is an extension beyond the earlier prophetic understanding from which the idea originally came. God's universal involvement in history and his Kingdom as a universal replacement for all other rule is a concept which was later incorporated in New Testament thought. In Daniel a time of destruction will precede the establishment of this everlasting Kingdom in which the persecuted—the saints and martyrs—will be caught up.

Finally, in Daniel there is the concept of individual resurrection from the dead for both the just and the unjust. By the time the book was written this article of faith had already gained wide popular acceptance. So for the author, salvation transcends the political limits and destiny of Israel and the boundaries of terrestrial existence. Here were intimations of a new dimension to the meaning of salvation, but it remained for Jesus and the Early Church to give these their fullest extension.

OUTLINE

COMMENTARY

STORIES AND DREAMS

Daniel 1:1—7:28

Daniel and His Friends (1:1-21)

The Situation in Life (1:1-7)

The third year of Jehoiakim's reign was not the year when Nebuchadnezzar captured the city of Jerusalem. It is a well-known fact that the city was not conquered while Jehoiakim was on the throne (II Kings 24:10-15). The confusion is understandable when we recognize that the author was writing in a much later era and took the reference in II Chronicles 36:5-8 more seriously than the historical records of Second Kings. Nebuchadnezzar, son of Nabopolassar, became king of all the Chaldean Empire in 605 B.C. upon the death of his father. His name is misspelled throughout the book with "n" appearing instead of the correct "r" (Nebuchadrezzar). This mistake has become so common in the modern day that Nebuchadnezzar is the most used form among those familiar with the era.

Judah was given into the hand of the Chaldean conqueror in 598 B.C. and was finally and utterly destroyed in 587 B.C. On the latter occasion the Jerusalem Temple was stripped and its sacred vessels carried to Babylon (see II Kings 24:18—25:30; Jer. 52). The name given to Babylonia ("the land of Shinar") shows the influence of Genesis, especially chapter 11, upon the Book of Daniel. Thus the Book of Daniel opens with the picture of exile in a strange, foreign land.

It was not uncommon for rulers to choose the well-favored from their prisoners of war for special training and service. Ashpenaz was ordered to institute such a program for the noble and royal prisoners in Babylon. Prerequisites for this privilege were very high. Youths chosen were to be of noble ancestry, without blemish, handsome, skillful in wisdom, endowed with knowledge, understanding in learning, and competent to serve the king. Those who qualified were to study the letters and language of the Chaldeans for a period of three years. Like Jehoiachin, those who were given special training would be privileged to eat from the royal table. Such privileges were probably highly prized and gratefully accepted by most of those fortunate enough to receive them.

Having sketched the general background of exile and having given the particular situation which arose within that context, the author with real dramatic restraint introduces the main characters. They are four in number, all Jews: Daniel, Hananiah, Misha-el, and Azariah. All were descendants of the tribe of Judah, and all the names contain some form of the name of Israel's God.

When these persons became part of the Chaldean court, they were given names befitting their new status in life. Daniel became "Belteshazzar," which means "protect the life of the prince." Hananiah is renamed "Shadrach," which is a corruption of the god-name "Marduk," while Misha-el becomes "Meshach," a name for which there is no present explanation. Azariah is hereafter called "Abednego," which is almost certainly a corruption of "Abed-Nebo" ("servant of Nebo"). These Jewish youths became part of the court, even as Joseph had become a functionary at the Egyptian court and Esther had become attached to the Persian royal house.

The Dietary Problem (1:8-16)

Jewish diet was a point at which friction inevitably arose in a foreign land or in an alien climate. Restrictions on foods were many and varied (see, for example, Deut. 12:23-28; 14:3-21; Lev. ch. 11). This was one of the areas of conflict which arose during the Maccabean revolt. Jewish faith was tested and loyalty was proved by fidelity to the dietary restrictions of the Law, because this part of the inheritance of faith was emblematic of the whole way of life.

The defilement which would come from eating nonkosher food became an immediate problem. Daniel made a rather daring suggestion to the chief eunuch. He asked that an alternative menu be provided, at least for a limited time; and God moved the eunuch to favor Daniel, as Potiphar had favored Joseph. Understandably the chief eunuch answered, "I fear lest my lord the king, who appointed your food and your drink, should see that you were in poorer condition than the youths who are of your own age." Should this happen, the tragic result for the chief eunuch would be plain: "So you would endanger my head with the king."

Daniel, always equal to the situation, said, "Test your servants for ten days." A vegetable diet was to be followed for a limited period and then the results were to be checked.

The experiment was acceptable to the chief of the eunuchs, and after ten days the four Jewish youths were far better in appearance than their non-Jewish companions. The steward, learning from the temporary experiment, made this diet a matter of permanent policy.

Success and Blessing (1:17-21)

For a generation for whom fidelity to dietary and other laws was a life-and-death decision, the success of Daniel was more than a charming story. To these youths who had been loyal God gave the blessings not only of good health but of wisdom and learning beyond their contemporaries. Even in a land famous for its wise men the king recognized the superior wisdom of these Jewish youths. The source of their wisdom was not culture, Chaldean or Hellenistic, but God himself. Such wisdom found its recorded form in the Law, and was the heritage of Israel. For the loyal and brave, God's support was sure and his wisdom available, as Daniel thus learned from experience. That experience stretched from the age of Nebuchadnezzar to the reign of Cyrus. Obviously the author by this story prepared the way for Daniel to appear in the next chapters as a wise man gifted especially in the interpretation of dreams.

Nebuchadnezzar's Dream (2:1-49)

The Dream of a King (2:1-11)

It is within the first verses of this chapter that the language shifts from Hebrew to Aramaic. The break comes with the beginning of verse 4 where the Hebrew text reads, "Then the Chaldeans said to the king in Aramaic" (see margin). The words "in Aramaic" are probably a note added later than the original writing to call the attention of the reader to the unexpected linguistic shift. Many explanations for this shift have been offered, but no completely satisfactory one has yet been made.

In ancient times it was not uncommon for kings to attach great importance to dreams and their mysterious content. This amounted to a kind of pre-Freudian dream analysis. Most courts had among the countless court officials and servants a large num-

ber of religious functionaries and magicians, whose primary task
was to interpret dreams. Nebuchadnezzar had such a professional
contingent available.

The introduction to chapter 2 indicates that the king was troubled in spirit because of his dreams and so summoned "the magicians, the enchanters, the sorcerers, and the Chaldeans," whose
functions at least on this occasion were identical. (Note that
"Chaldean" in this reference and elsewhere is a word meaning
"magicians" and not an ethnic term.) The dream interpreters
immediately asked the king to recount the dream, but the king
had forgotten it. In a fit of frustration the monarch accused his
befuddled magicians of stalling for time. He demanded with royal
finality that they recover the dream he had forgotten and then
interpret it or pay for failure with their lives. In utter despair
these wise men replied that no man living could do the thing
which the king required; only the gods were able to reveal the
secrets of men's minds and hearts.

Daniel the Interpreter (2:12-45)

The similarity between this whole chapter and the Joseph story
has already been mentioned (see Introduction). In both stories the
king's dream is interpreted by a king's prisoner, but in the Joseph
saga Pharaoh remembers what he dreamed. Moreover, the dreams
of Pharaoh concerned seven years of plenty and seven years of
famine in Egypt, whereas Nebuchadnezzar's dream encompassed
the kingdoms of this world and the Kingdom of God. In each
case, however, the effect was to save God's people from extinc-
tion (see Gen. 41).

Only after a decree had gone forth that all the wise men were
to be killed did the situation come to the attention of Daniel, who
by training was now classed among the wise men (see ch. 1). He
had taken the three years' course and now was a professional wise
man in the eyes of the king. Ari-och, the king's officer, was ready
to carry out the execution which had been ordered by the king
when Daniel inquired, "Why is the decree of the king so severe?"
Ari-och told Daniel the whole story, and at his own request Daniel was taken before the king so that he might be given an appointment to attempt the interpretation of the mysterious dream.
The appointment was made.

Daniel returned to his quarters and asked his three compatriots,
whose Jewish names are listed, to pray with him for the mercy of

the God of heaven concerning this mystery. The wise men earlier had said such knowledge was only from the gods; now Daniel sought to receive wisdom from the Source of all wisdom. A beautiful prayer of thanksgiving is recorded which ends with Daniel's awareness that God had made known to him the secret. Daniel, as the embodiment of the true Israel, is thus seen to share the true wisdom of God which was not known to the wisest of the wise. This incident of prayer understood in the context of the Maccabean situation is a clear call for trust in God's guiding hand. Furthermore, it is a continuing reminder of the need for prayer to the Source of all wisdom.

With confidence in the Lord, Daniel went to Ari-och and asked that the wise men not be destroyed, promising that he would explain to the king the whole forgotten dream.

Ari-och presented Daniel to the royal court and breathlessly announced that he had discovered among the exiles from Judah one who could interpret the king's dream. In his words to the king, Daniel made the point that no wise man could fulfill the king's demand. Not even Daniel could accomplish such a feat. "But," said Daniel, "there is a God in heaven who reveals mysteries, and he has made known to King Nebuchadnezzar what will be in the latter days." Daniel leaves no doubt that the source of all wisdom was with God but that God had shared that wisdom, and especially the vision of the future, with his people the Jews.

Daniel then recovered from the limbo of forgetfulness the repressed dream image and repeated it to the king. Some commentators have suggested that this image, with its four parts, is not to be compared with the four empires of chapter 7, since it is assumed that the whole image—all four empires—remained until the fall of the last. It takes a literalist of the first order to make this argument. A visionary, poetic soul was looking at the whole sweep of history, first in the form of a single colossus, and then in the form of four beasts; and in each case the point is that the kingdoms of this world were replaced by an everlasting Kingdom, a mountain that shall fill the earth.

Daniel, after customary obeisance and veneration, including expected royal honorifics (vss. 37-38), proceeded to interpret the strange dream which had been so disturbing. It is interesting to note that the author did not miss the opportunity to proclaim that God alone establishes rulers over men. God had given to Nebuchadnezzar a very great kingdom both in power and in extent. Following his empire there would arise in succession two inferior (silver and bronze) kingdoms. Finally, a fourth kingdom, powerful and cruel, would arise, but this would be a mixed realm made partly of iron and partly of clay. The iron gave firmness to the clay, but the kingdom would be a mixture of brittleness and resilience. In the end this impossible coalescence of iron with clay would fall apart.

When this happens, then God will establish his eternal Kingdom, which will fill the earth and replace all other rule and authority. It will break in pieces all other kingdoms, even as the rock which became a great mountain had done. The fact that this Kingdom will never be destroyed and that its sovereignty will never be transferred to another people is the central theme of the passage.

It is necessary to come to grips immediately with the identification of the four kingdoms, a subject of much speculation in the course of biblical study. The two most popular interpretations are:

First:	Gold	—Chaldean Empire
	Silver	—Media
	Brass	—Persia
	Iron and Clay	—Greece

Second:	Gold	—Chaldean Empire
	Silver	—Medo-Persian Empire
	Brass	—Greece
	Iron and Clay	—Rome

The first set of these identifications certainly fits the facts of the case much better than does the latter list. With few exceptions scholars are agreed that the head of gold is the empire of Nebuchadnezzar, as the text plainly states. The crux of the matter centers around the question of whether the identity of the fourth great empire is Greece or Rome. The facts of the case are these: Alexander the Great established a powerful empire which was torn asunder after his death. The Seleucids and the Ptolemies were a mixture, since at least two marriage alliances between their houses were consummated, though with tragic results. It is very clear in chapters 7 and 8, as well as in chapter 11, that the key figure against whom vengeance was sworn was Epiphanes, who was a Greek. When Rome replaced Greece as the great power in the world, it is understandable that early Christian interpreters or even pre-Christian Essenes substituted "Rome" for "Greece" in their interpretation. In a theological perspective they were correct, since Rome represented the same man-madness which possessed and destroyed Greece. However, historically Greece was the original target of the author in the Maccabean period.

After the destruction of the mixed kingdom, partly brittle and partly strong, God will establish his Kingdom without human aid. This Kingdom is to be everlasting and its permanent rulers are to be the saints. Daniel proclaimed that God would enter the arena of history to determine the outcome of the struggle. Although Daniel's time schedule was inexact, the Kingdom for which he looked has come and is coming in Jesus Christ.

Epilogue (2:46-49)

The conclusion of this passage is anticlimactic compared with the visionary grandeur and theological profundity of the previous material. Nebuchadnezzar bowed before Daniel and confessed his faith in God with these words: "Truly, your God is God of gods and Lord of kings, and a revealer of mysteries, for you have been able to reveal this mystery." High honors were given Daniel, who became chief of the wise men in a country known for its men of wisdom. Shadrach, Meshach, and Abednego were given good positions in the land, while Daniel remained at court. To those in dire peril whose lives were in jeopardy the story taught that God, who holds in his hands the destinies of nations and who will set up an everlasting Kingdom, had not forsaken them. The two-edged message, so typical of Daniel, is clearly given: strength for today and hope for the future.

The Fiery Furnace (3:1-30)

The Image and the Law (3:1-7)

Nebuchadnezzar set up a huge golden image of himself or of his favorite god, the image measuring sixty cubits by six cubits (90 x 9 feet). This monstrous idol was erected on the plain of Dura in the province of Babylon, where the king gathered his official family (satraps, prefects, governors, counselors, treasurers, justices, magistrates) to witness its dedication. The impression this colossus must have made upon people staggers the imagination. Having built the image and called the assembly, Nebuchadnezzar then gave orders that everyone should bow down to the image and that failure to do so would mean forfeiture of life itself. When the musical sound prescribed for times of worship in the Chaldean realm was heard, everyone bowed to the great idol.

There can be little doubt that the story shows veiled contempt for idol worship in any form, but special indignation is aimed at Antiochus IV, who demanded that the Jews be idolaters. Most of the people were so accustomed to conformity to the prevailing code of general behavior that they must have found it easy to obey this specific order.

Resistance of Three Men (3:8-25)

Verses 8-11 lead up to the point of this story. Malicious Chaldeans reported that conformity to the royal decree had not been universal. The Jews who had been appointed over provincial affairs of empire, Shadrach, Meshach, and Abednego, did not bow down at the prescribed time.

The three men were summarily hauled before the king. Nebuchadnezzar asked if they had indeed refused to bow down as he ordered. Before they could answer, he gave them another chance to fulfill the requirement and escape death in a fiery furnace. In spite of the somewhat formal style in which the story is now cast, the dramatic effect is not lost.

Shadrach, Meshach, and Abednego made a quick and confident answer. These heroes said that their God was able to deliver them from the death sentence. But then they added this significant and inspiring confession: "But if not, be it known to you, O king, that we will not serve your gods or worship the golden image which you have set up." Whether God would or would not deliver from immediate peril was not for these three the final proof of faith.

Religion too often becomes only a way of escape for men and women in danger. To provide escape from life's perils, however, is not the main purpose of God's dealing with man. Rather, the Almighty gives meaning to life. The author of Daniel stands on the edge of this great insight and lays the groundwork for later saints to know that *meaning,* not *escape,* is the chief product of faith. To submit to the degrading practice of idolatry was unthinkable because it would have taken away that meaning which made life worth living.

Enraged by the men's open refusal to honor royal authority, the monarch ordered that swift punishment be meted out. The statement that "the expression of his face was changed" means that the king's attitude changed from helpfulness to outraged dignity. So that there should be no doubt about the severity of the intended execution, the author adds the detail that the furnace was heated to seven times its usual heat. Furthermore, when the three Jews were cast into the flames, bound in their mantles, tunics, hats, and other clothing, the appointed executioners were slain by the heat. Humanly speaking there was no possibility of deliverance from the fiery furnace. The cause was hopeless.

Looking into the fire, the king was astonished to see with three men a fourth person "like a son of the gods." The three prisoners had been loosed from their bonds and no harm had come to them. This fourth figure was some kind of angelic being, sent to protect these heroes of faith from the terror of a fiery furnace (see vs. 28). To an age which had begun to wonder whether God was in fact with them in their distress, the author of Daniel proclaimed that God is always in the fiery furnace of man's need and is adequate for the most hopeless situation.

Epilogue: Protection and Deliverance (3:26-30)

Before the whole official family of the Chaldean Empire the three heroes were now ordered to come forth from the fiery furnace. The pagan king refers to them as "servants of the Most High God," a title which one would hardly expect from Nebuchadnezzar, whose sympathies historically were with his own national deities. Be that as it may, the three heroes stepped forth without hair singed or clothing scorched, and without even the smell of fire about them. The miracle of deliverance was so complete that Nebuchadnezzar, the most powerful of kings, blessed the God who was able to set his servants free. This is the second overt confession of faith by Nebuchadnezzar, but not the last (2:47).

Not only did Nebuchadnezzar confess his faith, he also supported that confession with a royal decree that any persons or groups speaking against the God of these Jewish heroes would be torn limb from limb and their houses destroyed. At the very least this amounts to toleration of the Jewish worship by Nebuchadnezzar, who is regarded as himself a believer. At the most it would imply establishment of the Jewish faith as the official religion of the Chaldean Empire. Neither of these situations came about in history. However, it is true that exiled Israel was extricated from the fiery furnace of Chaldean captivity when the people were set free by the hand of Cyrus, the Persian.

Only from the perspective of the Maccabean age could a writer deal so freely with Nebuchadnezzar, who was hardly a benefactor of the Jews. But the author's purpose was served well by traditions that Nebuchadnezzar recognized the superiority of the God of Israel. In the light of all this, the writer is asking, how can anyone take seriously the challenge of a ruler such as Antiochus Epiphanes? To men in every age the message is clear: no king can resist the power of God, who watches over and delivers his people in his own way and in his own time.

The Madness of Nebuchadnezzar (4:1-37)

Confession by Nebuchadnezzar (4:1-3)

This story depicts the king as a beneficent and friendly ruler, whose relationship with Belteshazzar (Daniel) and the Jewish community was most harmonious. Doubtless the narrative is drawn from a source much earlier than the Maccabean period, probably the neo-Babylonian period itself. Even in its present form it reflects neither tension nor conflict. Hence we may assume that it came out of the earlier period. Nevertheless, the material must have been thoroughly reworked to suit the purposes of the author.

Nebuchadnezzar addresses himself to "all peoples, nations, and languages" with the salutation: "Peace be multiplied." He is represented as a world ruler whose power is unlimited and whose will toward all men is "peace." His reason for this proclamation was to make known in humility "the signs and wonders that the Most High God" had wrought toward him. Having introduced the subject, the Chaldean ruler breaks into a poetic and lyrical confession of faith (vs. 3).

The Dream of the King (4:4-18)

The king explained how he had gained his understanding of and appreciation for the Most High God. Once more, as in chapter 2, a dream alarmed him, but on this occasion he remembered the content of the dream. As in the narrative recorded in chapter

2, the wisest of the wise were called to interpret, but none among them was able to give the needed interpretation. Finally, much to the relief of the king, Belteshazzar arrived to interpret the dream.

Having gone through the usual amenities, bestowing the expected compliments, the king related his dream. In substance it centered in a great tree in the center of the earth, reaching up to heaven, visible to the ends of the earth. Its leaves were beautiful and its fruit abundant, providing food for all. Under it the beasts of the field found shelter, and the birds roosted in its branches. This symbol of a great tree representing a vast empire is used also by Ezekiel in several places (see, for example, Ezek. 17 and 31). It also forms part of the background for Christ's parable of the mustard seed which became a huge tree (Matt. 13:31-32).

"A holy one"—that is, a heavenly "watcher"—came down from heaven with orders that the tree be cut down, its branches cut off, its leaves stripped, its fruit scattered, and that the animals and birds depart. These "watchers" are God's heavenly emissaries, frequently mentioned in the Qumran Scrolls.

Only a stump of the tree will be left with roots in the ground, but the stump will be bound. In verse 15 the stump suddenly becomes a person who is banished to dwell in the fields where dew shall gather upon him. His mind is to be changed from that of a man to that of a beast, which condition will last for seven years.

Nebuchadnezzar was told that the decree of heaven was made by God and delivered by "the watchers" to the end that the living should know that "the Most High rules the kingdom of men, and gives it to whom he will, and sets over it the lowliest of men." Of course this is the major message of the entire book, in stories and visions alike. Having related the substance of his dream, the king —showing strange humility for an oriental monarch—asked that Daniel interpret it for him.

Interpretation by Daniel (4:19-27)

Daniel spoke in most solicitous tones to Nebuchadnezzar, explaining that the dream, together with its interpretation, ought to be turned against the king's enemies. Repeating the long description of the huge tree, Daniel explained that the tree was Nebuchadnezzar himself: "It is you, O king, who have grown and become strong." Recounting how the watcher came from heaven with orders that the tree be cut down, the dream interpreter explained that Nebuchadnezzar would be driven from among men and would live as a beast of the field for seven years. But "the stump" would remain and the tree would grow back, after the king learned the lesson that "the Most High rules the kingdom of men, and gives it to whom he will." A call for Nebuchadnezzar's repentance completes the section, which was obviously written in its present form long after the Chaldean king ceased to be a flesh-and-blood person. In point of fact, the tradition about a king who returned to nature and to madness was circulated about Nabonidus, not about the great Chaldean emperor, Nebuchadnezzar. This tradition also came into written form long after the death of Nabonidus, but probably arose in oral form during his lifetime. It doubtless originated because of that ruler's frequent visits to the desert center of Tema. This section with the following fulfillment is probably directed in particular at Antiochus Epiphanes, who was popularly called Antiochus Epimanes ("madman").

Fulfillment (4:28-33)

After twelve months Nebuchadnezzar was surveying the splendor of Babylon while walking on the roof of his palace. The narrative in the next few verses is related not in the first but in the third person (see also vs. 19). With the egocentricity which goes with the divine right of kings Nebuchadnezzar looked at Babylon, ". . . which I have built by my mighty power as a royal residence and for the glory of my majesty." In fact, archaeology confirms the king's claim to be the builder of magnificent Babylon. According to this story his complete lack of humility before the true King of kings caused Nebuchadnezzar to be banished from his kingdom and made to live among the beasts of the field. His sentence continued until he learned that "the Most High rules the kingdom of men, and gives it to whom he will" (vss. 17, 25). The sentence is given and immediately carried out. Then with finality the author completes the action of the drama: "He was driven from among men, and ate grass like an ox, and his body was wet with the dew of heaven till his hair grew as long as eagles' feathers, and his nails were like birds' claws."

Actually Nabonidus, who ruled after Nebuchadnezzar, spent much of his time at Tema in the desert and was probably considered a "nature boy." Extra-biblical evidence from several sources confirms the fact that the story was originally told of Nabonidus. But the point here is that a man who tries to rule apart from or against God is mad. The Most High has power to reduce earth's most splendid king to the status of an ox and then restore him to his former glory. Antiochus Epiphanes was nothing in comparison with the great Nebuchadnezzar. Man's ultimate madness is the belief that he, man, is God.

The Resultant Sanity (4:34-37)

Even as madness arose on account of faulty faith, so sanity returned when faith came back in focus. Nebuchadnezzar lifted up his eyes "to heaven" and his sanity returned. What a contrast to the proud bravado recounted a few verses earlier, when he had walked upon a roof boasting in his own accomplishments apart from God! When his reason returned, he blessed the Most High "and praised and honored him who lives for ever." Then in a rare outburst of poetic beauty the author confessed his faith (vss. 34-35). After the king had become sane once more, he returned to the majesty and splendor of his kingdom. In fact, his kingdom was even greater than before. The obvious intent here is to demonstrate that so great a king as Nebuchadnezzar recognized and depended upon God's power, and that when this recognition of faith came his power was increased. The lesson is simple: human egotism always leads to madness, and simple trust is evermore the key to genuine sanity.

Belshazzar's Feast and Condemnation (5:1-31)

The Feast (5:1-9)

Feasts like the one held by Belshazzar for one thousand of his top lords and ladies were not uncommon in the ancient world. A tradition still lingers and is supported by considerable evidence that it was during such a drunken debauch that Cyrus conquered Babylon itself. This was done by the simple military tactic of diverting a river which flowed under the city's wall, after which it was easy enough to get inside the wall by walking on the dry bed of the stream.

The story of the feast is related to the general theme of the book, for during its progress the king ordered the captured sacred vessels from Jerusalem's Temple to be brought out. These vessels had been brought to Babylon by Nebuchadnezzar after his conquest of Judah. Since they were vessels for God, they were kept in the temple of Marduk at Babylon. It was from these sacred vessels that the guests at the banquet drank wine while praising idols of gold and silver, bronze, iron, wood, and stone. Thus Belshazzar committed the ultimate blasphemy, as did Antiochus Epiphanes in the days of the author.

During this sacrilege the fingers of a man's hand appeared and wrote, as the terrified king and his guests watched. In verse 6 there is a vivid description of the terror and fear which possessed the king, causing his face to blanch, his arms to grow weak, and his knees to knock together. Once more word went out to the Chaldeans, enchanters, and astrologers to interpret the strange event, even as Nebuchadnezzar had twice sought an interpreter for his dream (chs. 2 and 4). This time no threat was made, but a reward was promised to any who could successfully interpret the writing (5:7).

According to the pattern of previous experience and the story form utilized by the author, nobody capable of interpreting the writing could be found and the king was greatly distressed. It should be noted that the same story-form and plot are used in chapters 2 and 4.

Daniel Interprets the Writing (5:10-28)

There is a mild satirical note running throughout these stories. A Jew living in the land famous for its wise men was the only truly wise man, for his wisdom came from the Source of all learning—God himself.

The queen, hearing of her husband's discomfiture and distressed for him, remembered that Daniel, in whom "the spirit of the holy gods" dwelt, had been appointed chief of the Chaldeans by Nebuchadnezzar. She was convinced that this expert from among the Jews could unravel the meaning of the handwriting on the wall. So Daniel, the wisest of the wise, was summoned to appear before the king. The queen referred to Daniel by name and also remembered the name "Belteshazzar" given to this exiled Jew by Nebuchadnezzar himself.

In verses 13-16 there is a single statement made by the king to Daniel, wherein Belshazzar identifies Daniel with earlier days, explains what had happened and how the enchanters and Chaldeans had been unable to unravel the wonder of the handwriting, and finally promises that whoever succeeds in clearing up the mystery will be rewarded with high position in the kingdom. From a dramatic standpoint this repetition in direct discourse of material contained in the earlier sections is designed to set the stage for the next phase of the drama.

Daniel was not interested in the reward, and he made this fact clear to the king before proceeding to preach the king a sermon on the lesson of history. The fact that the Most High had given the kingdom into the hand of Nebuchadnezzar is repeated. In fact, the greatness of the Chaldean Empire and its authority over many peoples was, according to Daniel, explained only by the blessing of the Almighty, who is the author of all rule and authority.

The story of the pride which had brought temporary eclipse to the great king's power is retold as warning. It had been a lesson hard for Nebuchadnezzar to learn. Only after his mind was made like that of a beast and only after living like an animal of the field did he learn the central lesson of life and history that "the Most High God rules the kingdom of men, and sets over it whom he will" (vs. 21).

Turning from his reference to Nebuchadnezzar, the wise man from Israel warned Belshazzar. The experience of his grandfather, Nebuchadnezzar (see Introduction), had not taught Belshazzar the lesson of humility so necessary for God's continued favor (vss. 22-23).

The interpretation of the writing in verses 24-28 is a continuation of Daniel's speech which reviewed Nebuchadnezzar's experience and Belshazzar's unwillingness to learn the lesson of humility. It was on account of this unhappy case history that the hand had mysteriously written on the wall words difficult to interpret.

The writing was "MENE, MENE, TEKEL, and PARSIN." It has been suggested that these words were originally Babylonian weights— mina, shekel, and pares (a half-mina). It is also possible that these three words together were a familiar expression at that time. However, even if the words were numbers, the meaning went far beyond. The popular saying was used to carry a greater lesson.

"MENE" is interpreted to mean: "God has numbered the days of your kingdom and brought it to an end." The number of days had run out for Belshazzar and his end was at hand. Similarly, TEKEL means: "You have been weighed in the balances and found wanting." Having been weighed in the balances of God's judgment, Belshazzar stood under judgment and was already condemned. Finally, PERES is understood to mean: "Your kingdom is divided and given to the Medes and Persians." A play on words was a familiar pattern among the Hebrews; hence, it is not surprising to see PERES meaning "to divide" and at the same time calling attention to *Paras* or Persia. Belshazzar's city and kingdom did fall into the hands of Cyrus the Great, who was the inheritor of Persian and Median power. As an independent entity, however, the Medes who had aided in the destruction of Assyria in the late seventh century no longer existed.

Thus the writer drives home the predominant, recurrent theme of the book, that the dominions of men are always under the judgment of God, who alone gives or takes away all rule and authority. For Nebuchadnezzar madness was the way to true sanity, but Belshazzar was not so fortunate. His pride was the ultimate effrontery to God. To those suffering under the mad egotism of Antiochus IV this story pointed to the true ground for hope.

Reward and Punishment (5:29-31)

Belshazzar, true to his word, made Daniel the third ruler of the land with all honors appertaining thereto. Ahead of Daniel stood only Nabonidus and his regent son Belshazzar. Thus one loyal Hebrew, an example for all Israel, had not only come to be the wisest of the wise but also had been given a place of rule in a heathen land. The similarity to the Joseph stories is striking, even at the most cursory reading, yet there was probably little if any direct borrowing.

The next two verses have been a bone of contention among interpreters for years past. Who is Darius the Mede who took over Belshazzar's kingdom at the age of 62 years? Identification of Darius with various historical characters has been attempted but with little success. In fact, even if an identification could be solidly made, the implication that there was a Median dynasty between the Chaldean and the Persian empires would still remain a problem. There is, as we have already noted, no place in time for such a dynasty. Cyrus the Great, a Persian, conquered Babylon and became its king in 539 B.C.; this is a matter of well-authenticated history. "Darius the Mede" is doubtless a later remembrance of Darius the Great who ruled from 522 to 486 B.C. The major lesson of the chapter stands, however, irrespective of exactitude in historical framework. In point of fact the Chaldean Empire did disintegrate, and Daniel was proclaiming that any empire or quasi-empire built on the same false assumptions faced inevitable disintegration.

Daniel in the Lions' Den (6:1-28)

Daniel's Position in the Land (6:1-3)

Darius the Mede was ruler in a kingdom with 120 satraps governing over their allotted satrapies. The system of satrapies was set up by Darius I (522-486 B.C.), who was a Persian and not a Mede, and he set up 20, not 120. Later, in Darius' own records, 21, 23, and 29 satraps are mentioned. Over the 120 satraps specified in the Book of Daniel three presidents were assigned, and one of these was Daniel. The point of all this historical orientation is that Daniel, the Jew, held a very high position in the kingdom of Darius the Mede. Daniel was the king's administrative officer, whose task was to watch over one-third of the kingdom's interests so that there should be no misappropriation of the king's property. Daniel, like Joseph in the Genesis account, made such a good record that a promotion was in process; he was about to be elevated to the position of steward of the entire kingdom. Daniel, who had been made chief of the wise men under Nebuchadnezzar and the third ruler of the kingdom in Belshazzar's reign, was now on the verge of becoming royal prime minister for the whole kingdom.

Emperor Worship and Its Consequences (6:4-24)

The central section of this chapter is built on the same framework as chapter 3, with similar motifs, except that there the lives of three men were put in jeopardy because of their loyal love for the Lord. In the earlier chapter, worship of a great image was commanded; here worship of any other god except the king was forbidden. Except for these differences the two stories follow the same general pattern.

Enemies of Daniel, fearful of his power and jealous of his position, could find no fault in his conduct or his royal service. But then they remembered his loyalty to the Law of God, and said, "We shall not find any ground for complaint against this Daniel unless we find it in connection with the law of his God." "Law" as used here would include the whole Covenant tradition, together with devotional habits such as the prescription for daily prayer.

Going to the king, these officials, who were apparently afraid that Daniel's elevation would mean their elimination, suggested to the king that he should establish a decree for the whole kingdom: ". . . that whoever makes petition to any god or man for thirty days, except to you, O king, shall be cast into the den of lions." This kind of law honoring the king was a normal means of establishing unqualified allegiance to the king; that is to say, it was an ancient form of the loyalty oath.

These clever enemies asked that this proclamation be given the status of a law of the Medes and Persians, which could neither be changed nor compromised. To this the king, thankful for his loyal officers, agreed at once. The document was signed and the trap for Daniel was set.

The story makes it clear that Daniel did not pray in ignorance of the law; he prayed in defiance of the king's demand. This exiled Jew continued the regular pattern for prayer, facing Jerusalem and making prayer morning, noon, and night. The point of the story is simple: no human command may ever be allowed to cancel the command of God. When the State demands for itself that allegiance which belongs only to God, the State then stands under divine judgment.

The plotters reappeared before the king and asked him to confirm his earlier edict concerning worship. This he did without hesitation, repeating the absolute nature of the order. Once the king had thus confirmed the unalterable law, the plotters reported that Daniel had not done according to the king's will.

The king realized too late that he had been maneuvered into a cul-de-sac, from which he manfully tried to extricate himself in order to save his servant Daniel. The great king, however, was pointedly reminded that the law was unchangeable and must be carried out. Thus the drama is brought to its tensest moment.

Daniel was forthwith cast into a den of lions. In the span of a few short verses his lot has been changed from that of a man expecting a high position to that of a prisoner facing execution. Yet God, who made it possible for Daniel to rise to power, would also protect him from death because he had been loyal in prayer even under threat of death. For those living under the rule of Antiochus Epiphanes, where every evidence of piety or faith (for example, circumcision, the Law, sacrifice, prayer) was punishable by death, this story would be a powerful encouragement. Israel's greatness, like Daniel's, was a gift from God, not an attainment by man; hence Israel must at this moment remember that her redemption was dependent upon the same Deity.

This king, unlike the characters in earlier stories, was most regretful about the necessity which law had laid upon him, so he appealed to the authority which stood behind and beyond the law (vs. 16). He then spent the sleepless night fasting.

With the dawn it was discovered that Daniel had been delivered from the lions because he had been "found blameless" before God and the king. Righteousness was his sure defense and purity his armor. Obviously the King of kings had overruled the order of the earthly ruler, who was now free to set the prisoner at liberty. Man had carried out the sentence of human law, but God had thwarted its fulfillment. That a heathen king should refer to the Lord as the living God and could understand Daniel's loyalty gives us pause until we realize that the primary concern of the author was not historical fact but theological fact—the faith factor. Only the living God could redeem from such distress. This he would surely do for those who served him continually and were without fault. Later man was to learn in Jesus Christ that there are no perfect Daniels; rather, God the Father redeems those who are fault-ridden but who have been possessed by a great faith.

In order to make apparent the full lesson that righteousness prospers and wickedness must perish, the author recorded the horrible end of those who misled the king. Like Haman in the Book of Esther, they became victims of their own plot. It is true historically that any king of that ancient day who had been duped by his advisers would summarily have disposed of them and their families. This touch removes any doubt about the miraculous deliverance of Daniel because the lions, who did not touch him, immediately consumed the wicked.

Results (6:25-28)

Darius wrote a decree, in the form of a confession of faith in Daniel's God, that all citizens "tremble and fear before the God of Daniel" (vss. 26-27). It should be obvious that the whole story is a vehicle for the expression of faith and that this beautiful confession was put into the mouth of the king so that contemporary readers might know what kind of God it was whom they served. Were we to take Daniel literally, we should find it necessary to assume that the Chaldean Empire and the Median Empire were converted to Judaism. There is no evidence that this happened. But that God the Most High sets up and brings down the great empires of this world is impressively confirmed by history.

The last sentence of the chapter extends Daniel's life span into the reign of Cyrus the Persian. Thus his experience, having begun under Nebuchadnezzar, spans the reigns of Nabonidus, Belshazzar, Darius the Mede (?), and Cyrus the Great. To say the least, this constituted a long and illustrious life. Moreover, one who served in three of the four great kingdoms could well stand not only as example to Israel but also as proclaimer of Israel's true future.

Daniel's Dream of Four Beasts (7:1-28)

This chapter was probably once an independent literary piece which has now been attached to the earlier six chapters. It is parallel to chapter 2, where the four-empire theory was introduced by the dream of Nebuchadnezzar in which he saw an image of gold, silver, brass, and iron-clay.

The Dream Itself (7:1-14)

In the first year of Belshazzar, co-regent with his father Nabonidus, Daniel had a dream which had special significance. So that he would not forget the substance of the dream he made a written record of it. It is interesting to note that from this point forward in the book the material is mostly by Daniel and not about him, the narrative being generally preserved in the first person singular.

The "four winds of heaven" were thought to come from the four corners of the earth and "the great sea" is doubtless a double reference—to the Mediterranean and at the same time to the primeval deeps. The background for this whole vision is the struggle between chaos and cosmos which is depicted in Genesis and is a recurring motif throughout much of the Old Testament. It was thought that, if it were not for the restraining power of God, evil would break forth from the great deep (see, for example, Gen. 1:2; 7:11; Isa. 51:9-10; Amos 7:4).

Out of the turbulent sea emerged "four great beasts" who were "different from one another" (vs. 3); evil had come out of the sea to struggle with good. There is always the downward pull of confusion against order (see Rev. 13:1). It was with this understanding of the sea in mind that the writer of the Apocalypse predicted a time when there would be no more sea; that is, when the source of chaotic evil would be destroyed by God (Rev. 21:1).

The first beast was a lion with the wings of an eagle, thus combining the features of the rulers of land and air. This lion-eagle was made to stand upon its hind legs. Its wings were plucked off and it was given the mind of a man. The cryptic passage appears to refer to Nebuchadnezzar's madness and to the waning power of the Chaldean Empire in his latter years (vs. 4).

The second beast is like a ravenous bear, raised up on one side ready for attack, having in its mouth "three ribs." Ordinarily these three ribs have been identified with the remains of partly devoured prey which this beast had not finished consuming. However, an old proposal, which until recently had been discarded, has much to support it. On the basis of an Arabic word meaning "fangs, incisors," the three ribs may better be interpreted as "three large fangs." The correct translation, then, would be "three fangs were in its mouth." This bear with three large incisors among its teeth was ordered to "Arise, devour much flesh."

A third beast followed the bear. It was "like a leopard, with four wings of a bird on its back; and the beast had four heads; and dominion was given to it" (vs. 6). The four wings probably refer to the swiftness of conquest by this beast, while the four heads may refer to the four corners of the earth which were brought under Medo-Persian domination. The suggestion that the four heads refer to the best-known Persian rulers—Cyrus, Darius, Artaxerxes, and Xerxes—makes good sense. In any case, the third beast was swift and powerful, although not as great or as powerful as the first two.

Then Daniel records the climax of his night vision. "After this I saw . . . a fourth beast, terrible and dreadful and exceedingly strong; and it had great iron teeth; it devoured and broke in pieces, and stamped the residue with its feet. It was different from all the beasts that were before it; and it had ten horns" (vs. 7). This indescribable beast is obviously the most terrifying of all, and is by far the most cruel. Iron teeth that devour and break are indicative of the bestial nature of this monster. In ancient symbols it was not unusual for animals to have as many as ten horns; hence this picture was quite within the framework of accepted expression. "Horns" usually refer to rulers, which is the case in this passage.

Watching with transfixed interest these ten horns, Daniel was amazed to see "another horn, a little one, before which three of the first horns were plucked up by the roots." One ruler displaced three to gain the throne. The reference was to Antiochus Epiphanes, who had "a mouth speaking great things."

In this fashion a review of history beginning with the Chaldean era and leading to Antiochus passed before the eyes of Daniel. But for the man of God this was not the whole story. In fact, this was not even the important part of the historical scene, since history and life to be understood correctly must be viewed in the perspective of God. Daniel now saw the central feature of his vision (vss. 9-10). This theophany (appearance of God), though dependent for imagery on earlier visions, has a grandeur and a glory unique in biblical record. The scene is obviously a judgment scene where God was sitting in judgment upon the throne of his glory. The fact that the throne had wheels has an obvious relationship to Ezekiel's visions (Ezek. 1 and 10). Fiery flames and a stream of fire usually had a central place in theophanies (for example, Gen. 15; Exod. 3:2; 19:16-25; II Kings 2:10-12; Isa. 6:1-8). Fire combines the symbolism of judgment and of purification. White raiment was proof of purity, while white hair proclaimed that this was the God of all ages, no late comer. Uncounted multitudes stood in silent awe as the records of life and history were about to be opened. This pictorial vision of God and description of judgment became almost standard in the early years of the Church and is especially reflected throughout the Book of Revelation (see Rev. 5). It is important to remember that God's divine judgment can never be equated with the description of it. The reality is always beyond the power of the description.

At this awesome moment the little horn was speaking "great words," not realizing that the judgment of God was in process. As Daniel looked, the indescribable fourth beast was destroyed and given over to be burned. This is doubtless a reference to the dissolution of Alexander's empire. However, the rest of the beasts—lion, bear, and leopard—devoid of dominion, lived on for "a season and a time." There was apparently a belief that these kingdoms without power still remained in existence within the crumbling fourth empire.

The next act in the cosmic drama involved the judgment given by the Ancient of Days (vss. 13-14). The Ancient of Days sitting upon the judgment throne received "one like a son of man." That this was not just an earthly court is demonstrated by the "clouds of heaven" which seemed to uphold the throne. Referring to this passage, Jesus at his trial said to the high priest, "I tell you, hereafter you will see the Son of man seated at the right hand of Power, and coming on the clouds of heaven" (Matt. 26:64). In the Book of Daniel the "one like a son of man" "came" before the Ancient of Days; he is in no sense identified with God. He is rather the Ideal Israel, embodied in a person. Concepts of individuality and of corporate identity were so fluid that a single figure might easily have been understood simultaneously as both individual and corporate. In any case, the everlasting Kingdom was delivered into the hands of this one "like a son of man." Later in the chapter "the saints," who were God's true people, received the same Kingdom. Thus true Israel will inherit the Kingdom and the power.

Christian interpretation, which goes beyond the original intent of the author of Daniel, has always understood Christ to be the fulfillment of this passage. It was Jesus Christ who received the Kingdom which was and is an everlasting Kingdom.

Interpretation (7:15-27)

The four beasts are "four kings"—an expression which should be rendered "four kingdoms"—that would "arise out of the earth." In a symbolic sense the beasts came out of the primeval sea, the source of every dark evil, but in the historical sense they arose "out of the earth." These kingdoms are to be identified with Babylonia, Media, Persia, and Greece, although countless alternatives have been suggested. There is no great inconsistency between verses 2-3 and verse 17. These kingdoms will arise, but theirs will be a temporal and, as such, ephemeral rule. "The saints of the Most High shall receive the kingdom, and possess the kingdom for ever, for ever and ever." The "one like a son of man" mentioned above must be identified with the "saints of the Most High" in this passage since both are said to receive the Kingdom. The true Israel, the Messianic Community, shall inherit the Kingdom. It was Jesus Christ who fulfilled the mission of Israel and established the New Israel of faith. To these "saints of the Most High" the Kingdom will be given through Christ, the Son of Man.

The real center of gravity in this chapter is "the horn which had eyes and a mouth that spoke great things" (vs. 20). There can be little doubt about the identity of this little horn which sprang out of the indescribable beast; it was Antiochus Epiphanes. Apparently when this was written the repressive reform of Antiochus was in full swing. No proper offering was being made at the Temple. Massacre of all who refused to conform to the new way was actually in process. Against the true Israel who remained faithful to God, the "little horn" was at war. The conflict would continue until in judgment God gave the everlasting Kingdom into their hands, as had been divinely promised.

It is plain that the writer expected that the Kingdom would be given over to the righteous remnant in the immediate future. After Antiochus IV, the Kingdom would come. The author conceived of this everlasting dominion as about to be established on the earth in Palestine. Much of the confusion about the Kingdom and the Church today arises because of an unwillingness to see that these insights are partial, not final. When God's rule is complete, *de facto,* there must be a new heaven and a new earth.

In a statement cast in poetic form the fourth beast was identified as the fourth kingdom on earth, which would "devour the whole earth" (vs. 23). Alexander the Great established a kingdom which in a very true sense did devour the whole earth. As for "the ten horns," they were the kings who succeeded Alexander the Great but whose exact identity was of little importance at this point. After the ten had passed, another arose who would "put down three kings." The three displaced have been variously identified with a series of would-be royal trios. Be that as it may, the little horn came to power over all his opponents, whom he had either destroyed or displaced. His policy was to "speak words against the Most High," "wear out the saints of the Most High," and "change the times and the law." Antiochus IV thought that he was Zeus incarnate and was not at all reluctant to accept homage due to deity. He was zealous for the Greek way and instituted persecution to force the Jews to accept the enlightened culture of Greece. Death was the threat held over "the saints" who remained loyal to their heritage. In addition to other facets of reform, Antiochus sought to change the fixed times in Israel's worship and to blot out all knowledge of and obedience to the Law of God.

God allowed this time of bloody resistance to continue for "a time, two times, and half a time" or, in our modern way of reckoning, three and a half years. However, it should be remembered that this was a round number, being one half of seven, which was the most common Hebrew round number. To say "three and a half" at that time was similar to our saying "half-a-dozen." People were asking: How long? Daniel gave God's answer that the persecution and tribulation would continue for only three and a half years.

At the end of that time the heavenly court, as forecast in the earlier part of the dream, would meet, and the dominion of Antiochus would be taken away, consumed, and destroyed. Very shortly Antiochus did die. At this juncture in time "the greatness of the kingdoms under the whole heaven" was to be given to "the saints of the Most High." All rule and authority was to be given to "the saints" who had been loyal to the faith. New meaning was given to this passage in the light of Jesus Christ, whose coming ushered in the Kingdom of God, in which believers are citizens. The main lesson of the chapter is that although God may be allowing persecution to continue for a little while, his final aim is to give the Kingdom to the saints.

Postscript (7:28)

This single verse was probably the concluding verse of a larger section before materials from other sources were added to chapters 2-7. It tells us that Daniel was alarmed and that he kept his visions secret.

VISIONS AND PROMISE
Daniel 8:1—12:13

The last section of Daniel is more involved with the author's contemporary historical situation, especially with its pressures and its hopes. No long thrust back into the past is given except as background for the immediate present. Even the four-kingdom idea is truncated to a two-kingdom approach (Persia and Greece), but it is primarily one king who is the subject for scorn in these visions of the end-time. "Seventy weeks" are used to fill the gap between captivity and redemption for the Jews, and chapter 11 is given over almost entirely to a chronicle of relations between the Seleucids and the Ptolemies (see Introduction). Times and periods are estimated against the day when the present horror will be overcome and God's true reign will begin.

Vision of the Ram and the He-Goat (8:1-27)

The struggle between the upstart Macedonian king, Alexander, and the massive Persian Empire shook the ancient world. That struggle is dramatically retold here in the violence of a clash between a he-goat and a ram, symbols especially appropriate to the two empires in question.

The Setting (8:1-2)

Daniel tells where he was when this vision occurred and comments that it was after "the first," apparently meaning the vision recorded in chapter 7. He was in Susa, the great Persian center, during the third year of Belshazzar's reign, before the Persians came to power. The vision came while he was by the River Ulai. The author thus sets a cosmic drama of imperial conflict in Susa, which was the ancient capital of Persia, just at the time when the last vestige of Chaldean power was disappearing.

The Vision (8:3-14)

The River Ulai should probably be identified with a canal dug to connect the Choaspes and Corprates rivers, which flowed near Susa. This would parallel the situation of the River Chebar in Ezekiel, which is now firmly identified with the Canal Kebar. The ram who stood on the bank of the Canal Ulai had two great horns; "both horns were high, but one was higher than the other, and the higher one came up last." Media and Persia were the two horns of the ram, and Persia, the latter horn, was by far the higher of the two. In fact, Media never dominated the Near East as did Babylonia or Persia. The ram charging westward, northward, and southward at will, with nobody able to stop him, is an apt symbol of Persia's expansive power beginning with Cyrus.

While Daniel watched the invincible ram in all his magnificence, a "he-goat came from the west across the face of the whole earth, without touching the ground; and the goat had a conspicuous horn between his eyes." The unexpected appearance of Alexander the Great (336-323 B.C.) and the swiftness of his incredible conquest are meant. He moved so swiftly that his feet hardly touched the ground. Crossing the Hellespont in 334 B.C., Alexander made short work of destroying the Persian Empire by winning a decisive victory at Issus the next year, and by conquering unconquerable Tyre the year thereafter. When Alexander died in 323 B.C., he had brought the whole Middle East, from Egypt to the Indian frontier, under Greek influence and power. He was indeed the swift he-goat.

Verses 6-7 laconically tell of the brief struggle between the he-goat and the ram, which resulted in utter defeat for the once mighty ram. No ally or other power on earth could rescue the two-horned ram, because in its time of domination the Medo-

Persian Empire had made sure that all other centers of power were destroyed.

Verse 8 recounts how the he-goat magnified himself, but at the very height of his power his horn was broken. This reference is to the sudden death of Alexander the Great in 323 B.C. Instead of "the great horn" there arose four horns in its stead. Historically, after a period of struggle, the empire of Alexander was divided by four generals. Cassander held power in Greece, Lysimachus ruled over Anatolia, Syro-Mesopotamia was under the rule of Seleucus, and Egypt was controlled by Ptolemy. These are the "four conspicuous horns" which shared the heritage of Alexander's expansive domain and power.

The writer used broad, sweeping strokes to paint the background picture of cosmic struggle, but he wasted little time getting to the urgent present. Neither time nor space is spent on explanation or denunciation of the four successors or even upon the Seleucids and Ptolemies. "A little horn" appeared, which grew southward and eastward and, most important, "toward the glorious land," which was Palestine. This move toward Palestine is the disturbing center of the drama. The extent of Antiochus' intention is signified in the words, "It grew great, even to the host of heaven; and some of the host of the stars it cast down to the ground, and trampled upon them." This statement is not to be taken literally, yet Antiochus' egomania, expressed in his claims to deity, had such purpose in view.

The "little horn" magnified itself against "the Prince of the host," stopped burnt offerings, and overthrew the sanctuary. Antiochus did overthrow the high priest and replace normal worship with a Grecianized abomination. He took control of the Temple, which he apparently looted in 168 B.C., and for more than three years no proper offering was made there. The Temple was occupied and controlled by the heathen ruler. What was meant by "host" in verse 12 eludes us, unless it should be translated "temple service," thus reading with certain of the ancient translations: "And the temple service was given over to it together with continual burnt offering through transgression." Although we cannot be absolutely certain about the text, the meaning of the whole passage clearly points to interference with and interruption of Temple worship. "Truth was cast down to the ground" (vs. 12). True religion, as exemplified in the earlier stories, no longer had control because the little horn "acted and prospered." One senses in these passages not the atmosphere of what had happened or what was to happen but rather what was happening. This is the picture of the height of repressive measures in the early years of the Maccabean revolt (168-165 B.C.).

Daniel, having seen the shocking and almost hopeless state of affairs, heard a "holy one" (an angel) speaking to "another holy one" about the future. Doubtless the most urgent question among oppressed saints was: How long will this continue? That was exactly the question put by the one angel to the other. How long will this sacrilege, this blasphemy, and this persecution be allowed to continue? The answer was given as follows: "For two thousand and three hundred evenings and mornings; then the sanctuary shall be restored to its rightful state." This figure would amount to 1150 days, which is a shorter time than the three and a half years mentioned in chapter 7 (1278 days). It could be that chapter 8 is later than chapter 7, or perhaps we should understand both figures as round numbers or approximations. In any case the promised end of distress is clearly in sight, when rightful order shall be restored among God's people and in his Temple.

Interpretation (8:15-25)

The setting for the interpretation is so obviously related to Ezekiel 1-3 that there is little reason to pursue points of comparison. A voice spoke to Daniel, not directly but through the angel Gabriel, while Daniel was by the banks of the Ulai Canal. Like Ezekiel, this man of God was so overwhelmed by the experience that he fell to the ground (Ezek. 1:28—2:1). At this point the expression "son of man" (vs. 17) is used with exactly the same meaning that it has in Ezekiel, and should be translated simply "man" or "human being." Gabriel, having been sent by God, explained the vision: "Understand, O son of man, that the vision is for the time of the end."

A view of the end-time was given to Daniel after he had fallen into a very deep sleep. In this sleep the voice proceeded to tell Daniel "what shall be at the latter end of the indignation; for it pertains to the appointed time of the end." The consummation is the heart of the matter now. Media and Persia were the ram with two horns, and the king of Greece was the he-goat (vss. 20-21). The big horn was the first king of Greece. Actually Philip was the first in the Macedonian line, but his more influential and greater son, Alexander, was meant in this instance (vs. 21). The four horns are the four who arose to rule after the death of Alexander, as detailed above (vs. 22). At the "latter end" of Greek power "a king of bold countenance . . . shall arise." This was, of course, Antiochus Epiphanes, who is described as "one who understands riddles." The expression, "bold countenance," reflects the insolence and harshness which this "little horn" displayed toward God and man. The understanding of riddles is a caustic reference to his trickery in language and action in order to achieve the goals of his power.

His power would be great and would bring, in the wake of success, fearful destruction of mighty men and the saints of God. It was against this latter group, "the saints" who remained loyal and whose loyalty was remembered in the early stories of the book, that the heaviest blows of persecution fell. That Antiochus IV was a cunning and deceitful person is a well-remembered historical fact. Every device was used for his own ends because in his own mind he magnified his person to the level of deity.

To strike and to destroy without warning is typical of this kind of tyrant (vs. 25). Yet it is probable that this reference had a specific incident in view. In 168 B.C. the Syrian general, Appolonius, came in peace to the turbulent city of Jerusalem; but when all was quiet, he fell upon the helpless people and carried out a bloody massacre for the king (see I Macc. 1:29-32). The Temple was sacked and afterward Zeus instead of the Lord was worshiped there. This treachery was an unforgettable moment in the tragedy of Jewish history.

Finally the assurance is given that Antiochus will be broken by no human hand. It was a mountain which filled the earth that destroyed the image of four metals mentioned in chapter 2, and it was intervention by the Ancient of Days that brought an end to the beasts which foraged across the earth (ch. 7). Now the direct intervention of God himself will bring an end to the distress of his people. Only as God would enter the arena of history could there be sure hope. This writer opened vistas of hope which he could not fully explore, but which were finally fulfilled in Jesus Christ, God-come-to-man.

Postscript (8:26-27)

"The vision of the evenings and the mornings" is a label given to the vision because of the 2300 evenings and mornings which were the measure of its duration. This vision was ordered sealed and kept closed until a future time when its message would be relevant and needed.

The chapter ends with a statement of the effect that so overwhelming an experience had upon Daniel, physically and emotionally. He was appalled and baffled by the vision because he did not completely understand it. The author was now speaking in vision from the age of Chaldean power and saw the age in which he was living as being far in the future. In a dream he thrust himself back in time to get perspective for the present. The sealing of the book for future use must be understood from the vantage point of the dream, in which he stood in the Chaldean period. Thus an authentic ring of predictive prophecy adds authority to the proclamation.

Prophecy and Prayer (9:1-27)

Chapter 9 consists of three sections: a brief introduction, the prayer of Daniel, and the interpretation of Jeremiah's prophecy. The interpretation is the real center of this passage, which was expanded at some time by the addition of a beautiful liturgical prayer. Again the terminus toward which the "seventy weeks of years" (vs. 24) is made to move is the same center of gravity found in the two previous chapters, namely, the age of Antiochus Epiphanes. Alternate views have crowded the stage of biblical interpretation, but this one is transparently in line with the author's intent. Undoubtedly the original intent of this material was to interpret the era of tragic persecution, whatever the theological overtones may now be.

Jeremiah's Prophecy (9:1-2)

The date given here suggests the historical confusion which pervades the book because Darius the Mede is said to be the son of Ahasuerus (Xerxes). But Ahasuerus had no son named Darius. Darius I was the father of Xerxes, who was not a Mede but a Persian. It is certain, however, that the author meant to place this vision appropriately in 539 B.C. when Babylon was captured.

Reference to Jeremiah's prophecy of "seventy years" is the basis for a vision. Jeremiah had predicted that seventy years would pass while Judah remained desolate and her people were captive. After seventy years there would be restoration and revival (Jer.

25:11-12; 29:10). The author recalled this prophecy of hope and interpreted it as a light in the darkness of his contemporary world.

The Prayer (9:3-19)

Daniel's remarkable confession of sin and his petition for God's grace upon God's people is an outstanding example of prayer as practiced among the Jews. Whether this prayer was drawn from the liturgy of the Temple or that of the later synagogue is difficult to determine. It consists of well-known fragments of language and ideas drawn from various parts of the Jewish Scriptures (Ezra 9; Neh. 1 and 9; I Kings 3; Jer. 26; 32; 44) and is symbolic of true Israel at prayer in repentance for past failure and in petition for future recovery. Even though the prayer has literary affinities to several Old Testament and Intertestament passages, it still is an original work.

The reference to the Lord who keeps Covenant and shows loyal love to those who are loyal to him by keeping the commandments gets to the center and heart of the Covenant faith. This Covenant was instituted when by God's love Israel was chosen to be his peculiar people. These people were commissioned to display loyal love as a proper response to the action of God's love. God was a God of grace and of gentle love to those who kept his commandments (vs. 4).

The tragedy of ancient Judah was that while God remained a Covenant-keeping God, his people became a Covenant-breaking people, "turning aside from thy commandments" (vs. 5). Daniel recalled before the Almighty how the prophets were sent as God's emissaries to speak "to our kings, our princes, and our fathers, and to all the people of the land" (vs. 6). God had been perfectly righteous in his dealings, but "confusion of face" (shame or disgrace) had become the lot of Jerusalem, Judah, and Israel because of their treachery. All were now in captivity.

For these rebellious people there was no hope except in God's "mercy and forgiveness," because they had flagrantly transgressed God's laws and refused to heed his prophets. The statement that "All Israel has transgressed thy law and turned aside, refusing to obey thy voice" (vs. 11) emphasizes an undeniable fact about Hebrew history as witnessed by the prophets. Involved in the Law were the blessings and curses which people took upon themselves for obedience or disobedience (Lev. 26:14-25; Deut. 28:15-68). The curse prescribed in the Law of Moses had been fully poured out upon this rebellious people. God's words had been confirmed in history through the incomparable desolation which was visited upon Jerusalem (vs. 12). However, even the destructive force of God's judgment brought the people neither to entreaty for mercy nor to repentance for sin. For this reason the calamity continued (vs. 14).

Daniel, having set faith in the context of the Covenant and having confessed the sin of his people, began to make supplication for restoration. He asked God, "for thy own sake, O Lord, cause thy face to shine upon thy sanctuary, which is desolate." What more appropriate petition could be raised in the time when Antiochus had made the Temple desolate? The supplications of Daniel clearly are made not on the basis of human righteousness but through trust in divine mercy and forgiveness. Man can never plead forgiveness because of human righteousness; the ground must always be God's unchanging mercy. Finally Daniel reflects the concern that was frequently manifest in Ezekiel (see Ezek. 36), namely, "thy city and thy people are called by thy name." The Lord's honor and character appeared to be at stake in this situation.

The Angel Returns (9:20-23)

The angel Gabriel came as a messenger of God to give Daniel wisdom and understanding, so that he could "consider the word and understand the vision." Once more God is recognized as the Source of all true wisdom, in whom alone is the key to the future. However, this wisdom and revelation of the future had been given into the keeping of Daniel, who was himself symbolic of the faithful in Israel. The meaning of the seventy weeks is ready to be revealed to Daniel for safekeeping until the end-time.

The Seventy Years: An Interpretation (9:24-27)

The seven-year period of time was common in Hebrew thought, where the Year of Jubilee was to follow seven times seven years (see Lev. 25:1-12). The fiftieth year was the Year of Jubilee, while the seventh year in each cycle was the Sabbath year unto the Lord. Furthermore, the week-of-years (hebdomad) was relatively common, not only among the Hebrews but also among Greeks and Romans.

Taking the prediction that seventy years should pass before the end of punishment and exile, the Book of Daniel adjusts the meaning of the text to mean seventy weeks of years, which would total 490 years and would conveniently stretch from 587 B.C. to 168-165 B.C. Actually the times are not exact and should not be forced to fit into a precise pattern of dating. Should we require chronological precision the time of great distress would be reckoned as 96 B.C. Actually by starting from the center of gravity for this book, which has been demonstrated to be the early part of the Maccabean struggle, and working back to the time of captivity (587 B.C.), we should probably be following the author's intent. The result follows:

1. 7 weeks = 49 years, 587-538 B.C. (vs. 25).
2. 62 weeks = 432 years, 588-171 B.C.
3. 1 week = 7 years, 171-165 B.C.
   a. ½ week = 3½ years, 171-168 B.C.
   b. ½ week = 3½ years, 168-165 B.C.

"Seventy weeks," Daniel was told, would be required so that the transgression might be finished, sin ended, and iniquity atoned. Punishment and redemption would take time (vs. 24). Then the prophetic vision would be approved and the sanctuary anointed for renewed service.

Seven weeks of years were to pass before the coming of "an anointed one," who should be identified with the high priest Joshua. (From 587 to 538 B.C. there was neither anointed priest nor king in the land; only a priest was there after the Restoration.) For sixty-two weeks of years the city will be built up and its moat restored, but the years will be filled with trouble. No better description could be given of the Persian and early Greek periods than this—"a troubled time." After sixty-two weeks of years the anointed one will be cut off. Onias, the high priest who was deposed in favor of Jason in 175 B.C., was summarily murdered in 171-170 B.C., at the instigation of the high priest Menelaus (II Macc. 4:33-38). Soon thereafter, in 168 B.C., the sanctuary was destroyed, and the city lived in the shadow of a heathen fortress which Antiochus constructed (I Macc. 1:31-40; 2:7-13).

The usurper will make "a strong covenant" with many for one week. Antiochus IV attracted to him many Jews who were happy to accommodate faith and life to the new way (see I Macc. 1:11-15). These turncoats were bitterly resented among the pious in Israel. But for half the week—that is, approximately three and one-half years—all sacrifice was made to cease. This period should be identified with that time between 168 and 165 B.C. when all sacrifice was forbidden in the Temple, when the high priest did not serve, and when Zeus Olympus replaced the Lord as the object of devotion and loyalty. Supported by these abominations there shall come the "one who makes desolate." Antiochus IV was responsible for this sacrilege in the Temple. His defiance of God caused his Hebrew subjects to call him "Epimanes" (the madman), while his installation of Zeus Olympus was ridiculed in a pun meaning "abomination of desolation."

Once more the brilliant author of Daniel, a man of profound faith and unswerving loyalty, beheld God as the arbiter of all history, determining how long the desolation of the city should continue, allowing the time of trouble, and witnessing the final hours of terror. Ultimately this same God would bring to nought "the desolator" who had served a purpose in the divine economy.

Vision of the Last Days (10:1—12:13)

Introduction and Date (10:1)

The incident upon which this vision was based is set in the third year of the reign of Cyrus when "a word" (a message or a divine oracle) was given to Daniel, whose Babylonian name was Belteshazzar. The authentic word was one that spoke of great conflict. Daniel had some immediate understanding of the message and the accompanying vision. Thus three years after Cyrus conquered Babylon, Daniel is represented as seeing the whole panorama of history from Cyrus to Antiochus and beyond.

Setting (10:2-9)

Daniel was so affected by the dark pattern of the future that he immediately went into a "three weeks" period of mourning. Fasting meant that he forewent the usual delicacies, meats, and wines. Furthermore, he did not anoint himself with oil during the period of mourning. On the twenty-fourth day of the first month he was standing by the Tigris River. Once again the text is reminiscent of and dependent upon the vision of Ezekiel (Ezek. 1).

Daniel saw a man clothed in white linen, like the figure described in Ezekiel 9:2 (see also Ezek. 40:1-4). Some kind of emissary from God was intended. However, the description of this messenger from on high was patterned after Ezekiel's vision of God (Ezek. 1:26-28). His body was like beryl, his appearance was as a flash of lightning, and his eyes were like flaming torches. Although the language of Daniel is similar, unlike Ezekiel he does not claim to have seen the glory of the Lord.

Like Paul after him (Acts 9:7), only Daniel saw the vision, although a great trembling and an overpowering fear fell upon those who were with him. Fearful, Daniel's associates "fled to hide themselves," so that the author explains, "I was left alone . . . and no strength was left in me" (vs. 8). Completely enervated by the vision, the seer explains that the sound of words was too much and that in awe he fell upon his face on the ground. This is the pattern of ecstatic experience, vivid action followed by complete immobility.

Conversation with the Messenger (10:10-18)

God does not give his vision to men that they should lie groveling in the dust; having given his wisdom and strength, he demands that a man stand upright. So he had commanded Ezekiel; and now, like Ezekiel, Daniel was brought up trembling to hands and knees in a listening position. The angel spoke in most affectionate and familiar terms to Daniel, who was apparently no stranger. At the outset the messenger, probably Gabriel, reminded the seer that his standing was good in heaven. In fact, the angel admitted that he had come in answer to the prayer Daniel had made during his fast.

Gabriel had been delayed for three weeks because of a struggle with the king of Persia. Again the reader must understand the mode of expression in which earth's struggles were shadows cast by the conflicts among heavenly beings. The same view is especially evident in the Qumran community literature, known to us popularly as the Dead Sea Scrolls. Finally Michael, another angel, came to the aid of Gabriel, who was thus released to complete his visit with a message to Daniel. The writer is looking at history from the vantage point of God, a perspective in which Persia was a temporary and unimportant factor. The vision is still to make known the climax of the historical process (vs. 14b).

The clear literary dependence upon Ezekiel is evidence that this work came into its present form after the Book of Ezekiel was a well-known work. Like Ezekiel, Daniel fell to the ground and was dumb. Only by divine help did he surmount this dumbness (compare Ezek. 3:22-26). Proper humility on Daniel's part was quite manifest in his first words after the awe-inspiring vision. He had no strength or breath left in him (vss. 16-17).

God gave the seer strength to stand through "one having the appearance of a man." Along with the touch which brought strength, a voice was heard giving a word of encouragement. Having been given God's strength, his true servant Daniel was ready to hear the message. With this, the angel promised that he would return to take up the cudgels against Persia and then added, "and when I am through with him, lo, the prince of Greece will come." Before leaving to dispose of the Persians and the prince of the kingdom of Greece, the angel will reveal "what is inscribed in the book of truth." But first the seer must clearly understand that in this heavenly struggle only Michael, the patron angel of Israel, was an ally.

While this section of Daniel is strange to our thought patterns and conceptions of history, still it is the vehicle for profound insight into history. The ultimate issues of history are not decided *in* the realm of history but *above* history. The real battles are not the ones we see, nor are the actual powers the ones we behold.

Vision and Contemporary History (11:1-45)

Verse 1 is an introduction which seeks to fix the date in the first year of Darius the Mede. Actually the vision is a continuance of what began in chapter 10.

Verses 2-20 form a preamble to the career of Antiochus IV, who as always is the bestial villain of this piece. After Cyrus, "Behold, three more kings shall arise in Persia." These are a foreshortened dynasty of the great kings who ruled over Persia, namely, Darius I, Artaxerxes, and Xerxes. A fourth king, who is not easy to identify, but who is probably either Xerxes I or Darius III, will inherit such power and wealth that there will be envy among nations. It is possible that the prediction (vs. 2b) about stirring up "all against the kingdom of Greece" has specific reference to the Persian wars against Greece before the rise of Philip of Macedon. Afterward "a mighty king" shall arise to have great dominion. "And when he has arisen, his kingdom shall be broken" (vs. 4). So Alexander's kingdom was broken and was given to four successors, none of whom was rightful heir to his power (I Macc. 1:8-9). Like most of this chapter, these verses correctly chronicle actual history.

The king of the south (vs. 5) was Ptolemy I Soter (305-285 B.C.), who sheltered Seleucus I (312-280 B.C.), one of his princes, only to have the latter return to Antioch and gain power greater than that of Ptolemy himself. In fact, Seleucus I gained extensive control over the empire which Alexander's death left without a decisive ruler. "After some years they shall make an alliance" (vs. 6). About 250 B.C., Ptolemy II (285-246 B.C.) gave his daughter Berenice ("daughter of the king of the south") in marriage to Antiochus II (261-247 B.C.), but Antiochus had to put away his former wife Laodice to consummate the political alignment (vs. 6). Laodice, after a brief period, resumed living with her husband, succeeded in poisoning him, killed the child of Berenice, and finally disposed of Berenice herself. It is this blood-curdling sequence of events to which the writer refers (vs. 6).

Such treachery could not go without vengeance, which is described in three brief verses (7-9). The "branch from her roots" was Berenice's brother Ptolemy III, who marched northward in a very successful campaign which netted much booty, including "molten images" and "precious vessels of silver and of gold." For a brief period all was quiet, but then the king of the north, Seleucus II, tried a counterblow which met with only limited success.

Verses 10-19 deal with various aspects of and events in the reign of Antiochus III (223-187 B.C.), who is popularly known as Antiochus the Great. Antiochus, determined to wrest Palestine from the hands of the Ptolemies, came into the land in 219 B.C., when he scored great success. However, the threat of invasion spurred Ptolemy IV, who finally routed the Seleucid forces at Raphia in 217 B.C. Nevertheless, the words of the text are quite correct, "he shall not prevail," for Ptolemy IV was so impressed with his initial success that he did not follow it up (vs. 12).

After an interval of fourteen years Antiochus III, having regrouped his forces, came against the south again "with a great army and abundant supplies" (vs. 13). Meanwhile Ptolemy IV had been succeeded by the inept boy-king Ptolemy V. This made the task much easier for Antiochus. In those days there were also constantly recurring efforts to overthrow the Ptolemaic dynasty, but all failed. In any case, an attack was launched against Ptolemy V at Paneas, which was the last Ptolemaic stronghold in Palestine, and within two years (198 B.C.) "the glorious land" came under Seleucid control (vs. 16).

Antiochus III prepared to throw the full force of his kingdom against Egypt but, for reasons beyond our knowing, came to peace terms with Egypt in 197 B.C. (vs. 17). The treaty was sealed when Antiochus sent his daughter Cleopatra to be married to Ptolemy V. The intent behind the union was to use this marriage "to destroy the kingdom" by making it subservient to the Seleucid rule. This, however, did not eventuate because Cleopatra championed her husband's rule and urged the alliance with Rome against Syria (vs. 17). This was what the author meant by the cryptic expression, "it shall not stand or be to his advantage."

Fired with the desire for greatness, Antiochus III began a series of campaigns with a view to the conquest of "the coastlands" (196-191 B.C.). His ultimate target was Greece itself, whence Alexander had come, but the plan was not to succeed. Roman power was thrown decisively into battle at Thermopylae (191 B.C.) and at Magnesia (190 B.C.). Humiliated in defeat, Antiochus III did "stumble and fall" when, trying to sack a temple at Elymais, he was killed. Thus a reign of great glory came to an inglorious end (vss. 18-19).

Seleucus IV (187-175 B.C.) succeeded his father, but his reign was one of little significance; as the writer says, "he shall be broken, neither in anger nor in battle" (vs. 20). Reference here is to the historic fact that Seleucus was assassinated by Heliodorus, his finance minister and partner in crime, who turned on his master.

Having sketched the history of events leading to the rise of Antiochus IV, which at best formed a sorry chronicle, the writer turns to the point of this vision—namely, that the climax of wickedness in Antiochus IV is a forecast of the end-time. Antiochus IV was the "contemptible person to whom royal majesty has not been given" (vs. 21). The right of succession did not belong to Antiochus IV, who was younger than Demetrius, the son of Seleucus IV. By cunning and flattery, however, he succeeded in gaining power.

The text of verses 22-24 is uncertain at this point, but the intent is to show that Antiochus swept all opposition before him in Palestine, plundering and spoiling at will. In the words "but only for a time" Antiochus is warned and the people are promised that there has been a limitation set on this program of destruction.

Egyptian campaigns which were made by Antiochus IV are described in verses 25-30a. Trouble began between Egypt and Syria in 172 B.C. when two courtiers (Eulaeus and Lauaeus) seized power in Egypt and began plans to attack Antiochus IV. In 169 B.C. the attack came, but Antiochus IV won the battle and made Ptolemy VI his vassal king. Ptolemy's advisers were "his undoing" (vs. 26). The "two kings" are Ptolemy VI and Antiochus IV, who "speak lies at the same table, but to no avail." There was in neither the sincere desire for harmony or for peace, because Antiochus' chief purpose was to make Egypt a subject people and Egypt's motivation was to turn the tables. The ultimate outcome of history remained in hands greater than those of any earthly king and "the time appointed" had been set by God.

Returning to Jerusalem in the flush of success and "with great substance," Antiochus set himself against "the holy covenant," the Jewish faith, and plundered the sanctuary. Troops were stationed at the Temple, the place was sacked, and many Jews were massacred. This was done largely because a false report of Antiochus' death in Egypt led to the overthrow of Menelaus, who had replaced Jason as high priest. Upon his return, the king reinstated his choice for high priest and punished the rebels.

Once the situation was set right at home, Antiochus returned to Egypt for further campaigning, but in this second attempt fortune did not smile on him ("it shall not be this time as it was before"). "Ships of Kittim," which were Roman vessels under the command of Popilius Lasenas, forced Antiochus IV to retreat homeward (vs. 30). These same "Kittim" are mentioned in literature from the Dead Sea Scrolls, where they must also be identified as the Romans.

The time of horror began for the Jews when a defeated and frustrated would-be conqueror returned to his homeland. He immediately turned his energies to the major domestic problem, which was the fullest integration of the Jewish people into Greek life and customs (I Macc. 1:41-50). It was this determination which triggered the Maccabean revolt. Action "against the holy covenant" was the attempt to repress Jewish faith and life by persecution. In his effort Antiochus began to "give heed to those who forsake the holy covenant" and who thus became supporters of the newer Greek way of faith and life. "Forces from him shall appear and profane the temple and fortress, and shall take away the continual burnt offering" (vs. 31; see I Macc. 1:54-61). The general, Appolonius, on orders from Antiochus did capture Jerusalem, profane the Temple, and replace the regular ritual of offerings with Grecianized offerings and liturgies honoring Zeus Olympus, which in Jewish eyes was an "abomination that makes desolate" (vs. 31). Some Jews were seduced "with flattery" to support the new way, but the people who knew their God stood firm and took action (vs. 32; see I Macc. 1:10-15). Whether this action meant belligerent reaction, as epitomized by the Maccabees, or quiet withdrawal cannot be known (I Macc. 2:29-50).

The wise, like Daniel, "shall make many understand" the ultimate purpose of God, "though they shall fall by sword and flame, by captivity and plunder, for some days." When they fall they shall receive "a little help." This is a reference to the Maccabean revolt, begun by Mattathias in Modein in 168 B.C. (I Macc. 2:1-28). But this temporary revolt could not by definition be the ultimate source of aid, since that help could come from God only. Still there remained a division among the people—some choosing to join Antiochus and the new way, and others remaining wise and loyal unto death. The martyrdom of these saintly leaders served to refine and purge the community of the faithful, giving it a new purity ("to make them white"). But even this purging and cleansing by martyrdom must continue "until . . . the time appointed" (vs. 35).

Like so many tyrants, Antiochus IV was possessed by a god-complex. Daniel says of him that he would "magnify himself above every god, and . . . speak astonishing things against the God of gods." Even so, he would prosper in his mad thirst for power and divine status, yet only for a season. The same God who could enthrone or dethrone the great Nebuchadnezzar would find it a simple matter to deal with this contemptible and upstart ruler. Verse 37 bluntly states that Antiochus gave no heed to any god, neither the gods of his fathers nor "the one beloved by women" (Adonis), "for he shall magnify himself."

It is possible that "the god of fortresses" (vs. 38) may mean Jupiter, but it would appear more likely that the god of war in general was meant. Antiochus put his trust in his own divine power to wage successful war. The god "whom his fathers did not know" must be Jupiter Capitolinus, for whom Antiochus built a temple at Antioch, or Zeus Olympus, who was the head of the Greek pantheon. Both of these received homage from Antiochus at Jerusalem. By the help of one of these foreign gods he dealt with many fortresses, which fell before his attack. Those who agreed to his magnification of himself were given places of rulership, and among them the property was divided.

To this point in the chapter the author was actually recounting events which had already happened and was thus seeking to help his audience see the true meaning of these events in the light of God's sovereign rule. With verse 40 a change of perspective is introduced, because here the author begins to deal with the future and the substance of his message becomes predictive. Whereas in the earlier materials his only forecast was that God would remain in control and the time of distress would be limited, now the whole shape of the future becomes a matter for prophetic prediction.

The author foresaw another attack by "the king of the south," to which Antiochus, "the king of the north," would react with a rush of "chariots and horsemen, and with many ships." Although thousands will fall, Edom, Moab, and Ammon will escape the carnage which will engulf "the glorious land." These three traditional foes of Israel were employed to represent the heretics and turncoats who had gone over to the Greek way; they should in no way be interpreted literally. Those who were allied to the Greek cause would naturally escape the wrath of Antiochus' armed might. His rule is to extend over vast territory and his dominion will include Libya, Egypt, and Ethiopia (vs. 43). However, at the very peak of his power, news "from the east and the north shall alarm him" and he will go in fury to meet the threat at home. He shall pitch his tents between "the sea" (the Mediterranean) and "the glorious holy mountain," a location somewhere between Jerusalem's Temple and the sea (vs. 45). There the long-awaited end would come as predicted (Ezek. 39:4; Zech. 14:2; Isa. 14:25).

In point of fact Antiochus IV marched eastward into Parthia in the spring of 165 B.C. and during an extensive military campaign developed some kind of mental illness and died at Tabae, in Persia, in 163 B.C. The writer was apparently unaware of this exact pattern of events, but in general symbolic language he saw Antiochus IV on the verge of world dominion when trouble at home interrupted and prevented final success. His end came as predicted, even though the details of the prediction are not altogether exact. But what the author set out to do he had done, namely, demonstrate that Almighty God was still on the throne of history, making the decisions that would determine the ultimate course of history.

The Promise of Resurrection (12:1-4)

The reader must remember that the author of Daniel was writing while Antiochus IV was still alive and before the Temple was reclaimed and reconstituted for worship. In that perspective he saw beyond the "little horn" to the emergence of the Kingdom that would be delivered into the hands of the saints, to the Stone that would destroy the image and itself fill the whole earth. After Antiochus, the Kingdom of God would be delivered into the hands of the saints. Some people were dying in the holocaust and for them the urgent question arose, What is the basis for hope?

At the beginning of the end-time Michael, the patron angel of the Jews, will arise. Prior to his rise to power there will be an incomparable "time of trouble"; "but at that time your people shall be delivered, every one whose name shall be found written in the book." This promise is in effect an extension of the "righteous remnant" idea, wherein true Israel is only that portion of Israel which has been true to the Covenant. Many of the dead will rise out of the dust, the faithful to everlasting life and the faithless to everlasting contempt. The wise who have discerned the hand of God in the events of history, as Daniel did, and have remained loyal "shall shine like the brightness of the firmament; and those who turn many to righteousness, like the stars for ever and ever." With the dawning of God's Day of Judgment the wise man and the martyr will be raised to an involvement in life, freed from persecution and threat.

This same language and these same thought forms are carried into the New Testament language of faith. At the end-time when society is redeemed by God, it will not be as an impersonal or corporate mass, but as a unity of many persons drawn together in a single faith to which they had remained constantly loyal.

With his literary point of view still that of the Persian period, the author recounts how Daniel is to seal this ancient book until the time of crisis for which its message is meant. The book here sealed is the same kind of book whose seven seals are opened in Revelation (Rev. 5:1-5).

Epilogue (12:5-13)

The general thrust and intent of the treatise ended with the sealing of the book unto the end-time, but events demanded that some corrective footnotes be added for the sake of accuracy.

Once more on the bank of the river where the vision was first given, Daniel encountered the heavenly messenger, "the man clothed in linen," who was above the waters of the stream. Speaking for his people who were still caught in the grip of tribulation, Daniel asked the agonizing question: "How long shall it be till the end of these wonders?" It would appear that the glorious end forecast in chapters 7 and 8, as well as in 12:1-4, was still far in the future. The predicted period of three and a half years was not a satisfactory answer for those still in the fiery furnace of oppression. But still with both hands raised in solemn oath toward heaven the angelic messenger swears that the end will come after "a time, two times, and half a time" (see 7:25; 8:14).

The exact meaning of the next clause is uncertain. The shatterer of the holy people was Antiochus, who was the last manifestation of evil standing between the holy people and the New Kingdom. The shattering power aimed at the holy people will end, and that will be a signal for the consummation of God's promises. Daniel asked for further clarification of the future but was told, "Go your way." The words were shut and sealed in the book unto the time of the end, since they would not be fully understood until the end-time (vs. 9).

Meanwhile in the world the pattern of struggle would continue. "Many shall purify themselves, and make themselves white, and be refined." In trial and even by martyrdom, purity and cleansing will come to those who resist evil even unto death. But their resistance will not blot out evil because "the wicked shall do wickedly; and none of the wicked shall understand." To the wicked in any age, loyalty which faces death for faith or principle is never understandable. "But those who are wise shall understand." The wise who look at life and history with the eyes of faith see the goal of history and understand that life dedicated to God is not wasted when it is true even in the face of persecution.

Verses 11-12 are a kind of appendix to an epilogue which was probably added sometime later than verses 5-10. The urgent inquiry for an answer to the question "How long?" required more exactness, so the writer tried to provide it. "From the time that the continual burnt offering is taken away, and the abomination that makes desolate is set up, there shall be a thousand two hundred and ninety days." From December 25, 168 B.C., until the restoration there would be a 1290-day span of time. For no apparent reason the time is extended to 1335 days in the next verse.

It is possible that the starting point was different in each, but the important point to remember is that the end has been set within the limits of a relatively specific time. Again the point of faith was made that God had set the limits of the powers of men, for these powers are derived from the power of God and continue only upon divine sufferance. When God's purpose is done, man's tribulation will end and the instruments of that tribulation will be destroyed.

Verse 13 is a statement of tremendous beauty and promise. Not completely informed about the time span or the details of the end-time, Daniel was told, "But go your way till the end." Good advice this is in any time: Go about your normal business in simple trust until the end, which is in the hands of God. "You shall rest" may be a reference to the rest of death. But afterward the promise to Daniel is: "You . . . shall stand in your allotted place at the end of the days." Here, then, is the final confidence for the life of faith: seeing only in general terms the dimensions and details of our future, we go our way. God will cause us to stand up in our true being in the end-time. This confidence is the ground for hope when there is no hope. This attitude has been expanded into a major theme in much of the New Testament record. Daniel came out of turmoil and tribulation to speak to those who pass through these same experiences. But another came who said, "In the world you have tribulation; but be of good cheer, I have overcome the world" (John 16:33b).